JOHN
GOLDINGAY

※

THE
THEOLOGY
OF JEREMIAH

※

THE BOOK, THE MAN,
THE MESSAGE

Academic
An imprint of InterVarsity Press
Downers Grove, Illinois

InterVarsity Press
P.O. Box 1400, Downers Grove, IL 60515-1426
ivpress.com
email@ivpress.com

InterVarsity Press® is the book-publishing division of InterVarsity Christian Fellowship/USA®, a movement of students and faculty active on campus at hundreds of universities, colleges, and schools of nursing in the United States of America, and a member movement of the International Fellowship of Evangelical Students. For information about local and regional activities, visit intervarsity.org.

Scripture adapted from The First Testament *by John Goldingay. Copyright © 2018 by John Goldingay. Published by InterVarsity Press. All rights reserved worldwide.*

All New Testament Scripture quotations are the author's own translation.

Cover design and image composite: David Fassett
Interior design: Daniel van Loon
Images: gold texture background: © Katsumi Murouchi / Moment Collection / Getty Images
*   prophet Jeremiah fresco: © sedmak / iStock / Getty Images Plus*

ISBN 978-0-8308-5527-8 (print)
ISBN 978-0-8308-5528-5 (digital)

Printed in the United States of America ♾

InterVarsity Press is committed to ecological stewardship and to the conservation of natural resources in all our operations. This book was printed using sustainably sourced paper.

Library of Congress Cataloging-in-Publication Data
A catalog record for this book is available from the Library of Congress.

P	25	24	23	22	21	20	19	18	17	16	15	14	13	12	11	10	9	8	7	6	5	4	3	2	1
Y	37	36	35	34	33	32	31	30	29	28	27	26	25	24	23	22	21

CONTENTS

PREFACE

IF YOU'VE EVER TRIED READING THROUGH JEREMIAH, you may have felt that there are lots of trees but that you couldn't see the shape of a forest. Or you may have felt that the forest is full of examples of the same trees. Or, in contrast, you may have been mystified by the way Jeremiah can say things in one context that don't seem to fit with things he says in another context. Part of the explanation is that actually "the book of Jeremiah" isn't really a "book" in our sense but something more like a collection of blogposts. From now on, I'm going to refer to it as "the Jeremiah scroll," in the hope that this description may help us not to have misleading expectations of it. I hope to point to paths through the forest in a number of ways.

Part one introduces the scroll, looks at its origin, and introduces the man whose name it bears; it surveys the story that the scroll covers; and it works through the scroll section by section, focusing on a theme raised at the beginning of each section.

Part two stands back and considers what theology emerges from the scroll as a whole, looking at what we learn about God, about Israel as the people of God, about the nature of wrongdoing, about what it means to be a prophet, and about Jeremiah's threats and promises concerning the future.

The scriptural translations are adapted from my version in *The First Testament: A New Translation*, published by InterVarsity Press. I am grateful to Kathleen Scott Goldingay for reading the manuscript and commenting on things.

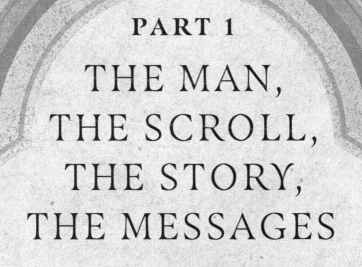

PART 1

THE MAN, THE SCROLL, THE STORY, THE MESSAGES

We get to know more about Jeremiah as a person than we do about other prophets, and that feature of the scroll has often attracted people. But the Jeremiah scroll is not his life story. Talking about him provides a way into talking about what Yahweh is doing with Judah and what Judah is doing with Yahweh. And the scroll is organized in a way that helps people understand what Yahweh was doing with Judah and what Judah was doing with Yahweh.

CHAPTER ONE

THE MAN AND THE SCROLL

THEY SAY YOU NEED a gripping first sentence if you want to get people's attention. I'm not sure that the first sentence of the scroll counts:

> The words of Jeremiah ben Hilkiah, one of the priests of Anathoth in the Benjamin region, to whom Yahweh's word came in the days of Josiah ben Amon King of Judah in the thirteenth year of his reign, and came in the days of Jehoiakim ben Josiah King of Judah, until the end of the eleventh year of Zedekiah ben Josiah King of Judah, until Jerusalem's exile in the fifth month. (Jer 1:1-3)

Whether or not it's gripping, it does tell us something about the man and the times and the scroll's origins.

JEREMIAH THE MAN

Jeremiah came from a priestly family in Anathoth, a small town three miles north of Jerusalem (the name survives as the name of a Palestinian town called Anata). Different priestly families were based in different towns— they were thus able to look after their land and livestock there and make their livelihood; the priests would go to Jerusalem when it was their turn to be on duty in the temple. They might also engage in teaching and counseling in their home area and be on duty at the local shrine when there was one. When Jeremiah lived in Anathoth he was within easy commuting distance of Jerusalem.

He calls himself a young man when God commissions him as a prophet (Jer 1:6), so maybe he hadn't reached the age to be a priest himself (thirty according to Numbers 4). And by the time he was old enough, for a variety of reasons the question might not arise. But he was someone well schooled in proper Israelite faith, and maybe his priestly father and his mother get a fair amount of the credit. He came from the kind of family that John the Baptizer would come from: Hilkiah and his wife were like Zechariah and Elizabeth.

On the other hand, although Anathoth was near Jerusalem, it was outside Judah in the region belonging to Benjamin. So Jeremiah would be a bit like someone from out of state living in Texas or California, or someone from England living in Scotland. He might not be viewed as really belonging and he might not feel he really belonged. Yet these dynamics were evidently complicated, as the scroll indicates that there was tension between Jeremiah and the people in Anathoth itself.

That first sentence (Jer 1:1-3) tells us that the scroll will comprise "the words of Jeremiah," which also express "Yahweh's word." The plural *words* points toward Jeremiah's addressing of a range of issues in different situations. The Jeremiah scroll is the longest book in the Bible apart from Psalms, and it speaks in different ways in different contexts. Is Yahweh going to impose terrible redress on Judah, or is he going to restore and bless Judah? Does Yahweh totally dismiss the temple and its worship, or does he affirm the temple and its worship as aspects of the ongoing life of Israel? Is Judah's devastation inevitable, or can it be obviated if people turn back to Yahweh? The Jeremiah scroll gives both sorts of answers to such questions in different contexts. But the singular *word* points toward there being a coherence and unity about the "words." They are all aspects of one "word."

There's another bit of complementarity. They are *Jeremiah's* words but they are *Yahweh's* word. Yahweh is the name of God in the First Testament, a bit like the way Jesus is the name of Christ in the New Testament. Most English translations replace the name Yahweh with the expression "the Lord" (they use capital letters so you can see what they are doing). But in Jeremiah, for instance, it's often important that Jeremiah is talking about *Yahweh* being the real God; someone like Marduk is not the real God. So I use the name Yahweh when Jeremiah does. Jeremiah's words were all concrete expressions of Yahweh's one word.

That word "came to" Jeremiah. Literally, it "happened" to him. Jeremiah uses the same expression when he declares that "Yahweh's word came to me"

(Jer 1:4), and it recurs often in the scroll. In some ways, Yahweh's word coming to him could be like another human being speaking to him, like hearing a voice behind him. Presumably the words were not literally audible; nobody else would have heard them, otherwise it might have been easier to convince people that it really was God speaking. But Jeremiah knew the message was coming to him. Even when he formulated the words, he didn't make up the message. It was Yahweh who gave him his overall perspective on Judah, his awareness that Yahweh was going to bring disaster to it because of its rebellion, and his conviction that in due course Yahweh would restore his people. And it was Yahweh who was behind his individual messages.

THE LIFE AND THE TIMES

There's a further subtlety to that introduction (Jer 1:1-3). While the Jeremiah scroll comprises the word of Yahweh, the words of Jeremiah, it incorporates many stories about Jeremiah, even bits of narrative in which Jeremiah doesn't appear, and prayers that Jeremiah prays that Yahweh sometimes rejects. Yahweh's word is bigger than simply a series of prophecies. The message is expressed in prophecies, stories, prayers, and protests.

Jeremiah's life as well as his words express his message. In a sense that's true about every servant of God, but it's true of Jeremiah in a way that's unique, until it becomes even more true of Jesus. Jesus is going to be an embodiment of God's gracefulness and truthfulness; Jeremiah is already an embodiment of them. He keeps being faithful to God's commission and he keeps embodying God's faithfulness to his own people. His life is also an expression of the message in a way that's not so voluntary, in that the negative way people treat Jeremiah is the negative way they are treating God.

The scroll includes examples of Jeremiah's prayers and protests to God, and in a modern Western context they are the aspect of the scroll that especially appeals to people. Reading Jeremiah's prayers and protests is like reading his spiritual journal. But the prayers and protests are in the scroll because they are part of "Yahweh's word." They reflect how the community is resisting Yahweh's message. They face us with what can go on between us and God as we are people who resist what God has to say to us. In this respect, too, the Jeremiah scroll parallels the Jesus story. We like to think that we identify with Jeremiah and with Jesus, or at least with Jeremiah's disciples and the Gospel writers. Actually, we are wise to see ourselves as more like the people who oppose Jeremiah and oppose Jesus.

The introduction to the scroll indicates how Jeremiah lived and worked over a number of decades in a tumultuous time. Northern Israel (Ephraim) had been overrun by the Assyrians a century before, so "Israel" now more or less comprised only "Judah," occupying an area that was for practical purposes smaller than Rhode Island. It centered on Jerusalem, and Jeremiah could speak of "Judah" and "Jerusalem" as if they are almost the same thing. The scroll's introduction mentions Josiah, Jehoiakim, and Zedekiah, the three long-lasting kings of Judah between 640 and 587 (there were two others in between, Jehoahaz and Jehoiachin, who reigned for only three months each, but the introduction ignores them).

- Josiah came to the throne at a time when Judah had long been a fringe part of the Assyrian empire, but when Assyria was in decline and a power vacuum was developing in the Middle East. He reigned from 640 to 609 (Jeremiah received his commission in 626). He came to the throne when Judah was averse to taking much notice of what Israelite faith really involved, and he took some firm action to bring about a reformation.
- Jehoakim (Josiah's son) came to the throne at a time when Babylon was emerging as the next major power, and he wasn't interested in maintaining his father's religious policies. He reigned from 609 to 597.
- Zedekiah (also Josiah's son) was put on the throne by the Babylonians, but he collaborated with Judah's desire to be independent of Babylon. He paid the price when the Babylonians besieged Jerusalem and destroyed the city in 587.

The city's "exile" didn't mean 587 was the end of Jeremiah's work. He continued bringing Yahweh's message to survivors of the catastrophe for at least a year or two. And the existence of the introduction and of the scroll itself indicates that there were people who lived on and were in a position to write about Jeremiah. The scroll thus collects messages Jeremiah gave (and stories about him and prayers he prayed) over some forty years in different contexts. Oddly, you might think, it doesn't often tell you what the contexts are—that is, most of Jeremiah's messages have no dates attached. It's possible to speculate about their dates, but it is simply speculation. Apparently we can learn from the messages and the stories without knowing their dates.

THE CATASTROPHE AND AFTERWARDS

"The exile of Jerusalem" was more literally "the fall of Jerusalem" or "the destruction of Jerusalem." It didn't mean that the city's entire population was taken off in a forced migration (Jeremiah 52 says that only 832 people were taken off in 587). But the word *exile* does suggest a great calamity, and there's no doubt that it was a catastrophe. The city's walls were demolished, its buildings were burned down, and its temple was devastated. Nobody much was going to be able to live there.

In English Bibles, Jeremiah leads into Lamentations, which comprises five prayer-poems that grieve over the fall of Jerusalem. Here's what it seemed like to people:

> Oh!—the city sits alone
> > that abounded with a people.
> She became like a widow,
> > she who was great among the nations. . . .
>
> Though it's nothing to you, all you who pass along the road,
> > heed and look.
> Is there any pain like my pain,
> > which was dealt out to me,
> When Yahweh made me suffer
> > on the day of his angry blazing? . . .
>
> Zion spread out her hands;
> > she has no comforter. (Lam 1:1, 12, 17)

While Lamentations is in a sense protesting, in another sense it knows it can't complain. It goes on:

> Yahweh is in the right,
> > because I rebelled against his bidding. (Lam 1:18)

Tradition came to ascribe Lamentations to Jeremiah, though like most of the Scriptures, it doesn't tell us who wrote it. But the tradition was on to something in the sense that the convictions expressed in Lamentations are broadly the same convictions as Jeremiah expresses. And much of the time, Jeremiah speaks in similar poetry to Lamentations. The messages, the prayers, and the protests use metaphors and similes and thus appeal to the imagination. And they mostly come in short, two-line sentences in which the second line completes, restates, explains, or contrasts the first line (this arrangement is called parallelism, though it's not a very illuminating description). Jeremiah's first words in the scroll provide an example. "Yahweh's word came to me," he says:

Before I formed you in the womb I acknowledged you,
    before you went out from the womb I made you sacred. (Jer 1:4-5)

Thus Jeremiah introduces himself. But this self-introduction follows that earlier one (Jer 1:1-3) in which someone else introduces him. And throughout the scroll there are sections where it says "Yahweh's word came to me" and sections where it says "Yahweh's word came to Jeremiah." There are stories about what happened to "Jeremiah" and stories about what happened to "me." The next to last chapter closes with the statement "as far as here it is the words of Jeremiah" (Jer 51:64) after which there is an account of the fall of Jerusalem and of the release of King Jehoiachin in Babylon in 562. Jeremiah could only have added that paragraph if he was about ninety. So the nature of the Jeremiah scroll makes clear that Jeremiah himself didn't produce it. Some other people, whom you could call his disciples, collected his messages and told his story, and his relationship with the Jeremiah scroll is a bit like Jesus's relationship to the Gospels.

WHO DID IT?

If it wasn't Jeremiah who produced the Jeremiah scroll, who was it? Actually, nobody knows. Its authors are anonymous, like the authors of Lamentations. Really, *authors* is the wrong word. They were people who looked after Jeremiah's message, put it into an ordered form, pointed out its significance to people who might read the scroll, and told the stories about him. Like the authors of Matthew and Mark, they don't tell us who they are. They want to put the focus on Jeremiah, not on themselves. I call them Jeremiah's curators and storytellers. They did their work sometime after the fall of Jerusalem, but their work then continued for some time, at least until the release of Jehoiachin in 562. One indication is that there is considerable difference between the version of the scroll in the Hebrew Bible and the version that was translated into Greek and appears in the Septuagint—much more difference than is the case with (say) Isaiah or Ezekiel. The Greek version is more than a tenth shorter than the Hebrew, and it has the prophecies about foreign nations in the middle of the book rather than near the end.

So much seems certain. Beyond that, it's mostly guesswork. For two thousand years scholars studying the different books in the Bible have had different opinions about questions such as who wrote them or when they were written, and that dynamic applies to Jeremiah as it does to other books. In our time, many of the scholars who are making waves in the study of Jeremiah aim to peel off layers in the stories and messages to get to earlier versions of them. They are inclined to note how the scroll incorporates different views on some key questions (for instance, whether God is going to cast off Judah finally, or whether he is going to restore the people) and how the story in Ezra 1–6 indicates that the Jerusalem community sometime after Jeremiah's day lived with tensions between different groups, like (say) the church in the United States. One might therefore be able to relate the different views in the scroll to the convictions of different groups. Working with this view generates various theories about how the scroll came into existence sometime in the next century or two, including the period covered by Ezra and Nehemiah—or later, when it was part of a Hellenistic Empire.

I take the more old-fashioned view that the scroll was produced during the decades soon after the fall of Jerusalem, during or just after Jeremiah's lifetime. I don't think the different angles that appear within the scroll need suggest authors with conflicting convictions, though even if they do, I don't see the process requiring a long time-gap after 587. The development of the two versions of the scroll might be later, but in general the scroll's language fits, for example, Kings (which was written during or just after Jeremiah's lifetime) rather than Chronicles (a new version of the same story, written maybe a couple of centuries later). Whereas the book of Isaiah mentions events long after Isaiah's day, the Jeremiah scroll makes no such references and focuses predominantly on God's critique of Judah and threats to Judah much more than Isaiah does. The linking with tensions in the later community requires a lot of connecting of dots, whereas the scroll's concrete references to peoples and events (specifically, the Medes and their underlings) imply the situation in the period before 539 when Babylon was the imperial power, not the subsequent period when Persia had taken over.

So I picture people whom in a loose sense you could call Jeremiah's disciples assembling collections of his messages, updating them and applying them to people in their day, and telling and reworking stories about him (like the Gospel writers). The process went on until the 550s or 540s, maybe in Egypt (where Jeremiah had ended up), maybe in Babylon (where influential exiles lived), or maybe in Judah (where there was an ongoing Judahite community). People thus carried on developing versions of the scroll, as people carried on writing the Gospels (Mark, then Matthew . . .). The scroll's two editions thus resulted from the communities' sharing of the scroll over subsequent decades.

There is more information on these different possibilities in the works listed in the "Further Reading" section at the end of this book. I'll sometimes refer to "the Jeremiah scroll" without necessarily implying that the words are not Jeremiah's, and I'll sometimes refer just to "Jeremiah" without necessarily implying that the words came from him rather than from a curator.

READING JEREMIAH FORWARDS

So from time to time, God would give Jeremiah a message to pass on to Judah. Maybe he would have a sense of having received the actual words, or maybe he would be more involved in formulating the words to express what he knew God wanted him to say. He might have been living in Anathoth or he might have been living in Jerusalem. He would take the long or the short walk up to the temple in Jerusalem, when he knew that people would be present for a feast occasion or a fast occasion, or maybe at an ordinary time when there would still be people there who had come to pray or offer a sacrifice or give thanks for something or just to hang about and talk because the temple courtyards were an open space where people could come. And there he would declaim his message. Maybe the message would be a couple of what we call the verses in the scroll, or maybe it would be more like a dozen. Perhaps it would lead into discussions with people or remonstrations from people who disagreed with him. And eventually he would go home. But people took little notice and they didn't change their ways.

But after the "exile" of Jerusalem, there were people who made sure that his messages didn't get lost. We don't get any indication that more people took notice of his message after that "exile" than before, but evidently there were some who knew that the catastrophe indicated that he had been right, and they included the people who became his curators and storytellers. The messages from Yahweh that he had given spelled out why the catastrophe had happened, how Jerusalem had "rebelled against his bidding" (Lam 1:18). So one significance of the Jeremiah scroll is to be an act of confession. It says, "This is what Yahweh said to us, and what we ignored, so it explains the mess we're in." In addition, it says, "You really, really, really better take note of this message now if you want to see Yahweh restore us as a people and fulfill the promises that he also gave us through Jeremiah." It also says, "You really, really, really better take note of this message now if you want to make sure that such a catastrophe doesn't happen again."

These curators more or less succeeded, in the company of colleagues who were doing the same curating with the history told in Genesis to Kings and with the scrolls that preserved the messages of prophets such as Isaiah and Ezekiel. Like theirs, Jeremiah's critique confronted Judah over the central features of Yahweh's expectations. You could see it as centering on the first four of the Ten Commandments (though we will see that Jeremiah takes up other questions as well). They talk about serving him alone and looking to him alone, not making images of him, not applying his name to the wrong things, and observing the Sabbath. Judah gets much closer to those commitments after Jeremiah's day than it did before. The curators were more successful than Jeremiah was. Or Jeremiah was more successful after his death than during his life. My wife Kathleen comments: that goes for just about everyone in the Bible, doesn't it?

Over the decades when it was his job to confront Judah about its rebellion and warn it about the disaster that threatened, it hadn't been his job to talk very positively about the future, which was the focus of prophets such as Hananiah (e.g., Jer 28). But he did some talk of that kind, maybe when the disaster was in the midst of happening and in the aftermath, so his message does give people some basis for hope. And not long after his death, his promises saw some fulfillment. People were able to rebuild the temple and eventually rebuild the city. Their relationship with Yahweh got going again.

JEREMIAH 1–25

Halfway through his time as a prophet, in 604, God told Jeremiah to write all his messages down. It was an important year, the year Nebuchadrezzar became the Babylonian king. (Whereas the First Testament—in English translations—mostly calls the Babylonian king Nebuchadnezzar, in Jeremiah the name usually comes with an *r* in the middle, so we will normally use the form Nebuchadrezzar.) Jeremiah 36 tells the story; its implication is that he'd never previously put any of his messages in writing but that he could remember them all. When I listen to singer-songwriters, I'm amazed at their ability to remember the words of all their songs. Evidently Jeremiah could do it too. Yahweh's hope was that confronting the community in those temple courtyards with an entire scroll-full of messages might pull them toward the response they didn't give to a message comprising a few verses. Some hope. The king simply burned the scroll.

I like the idea that Jeremiah 2–6 is the scroll Jeremiah dictated in 604, maybe with some bits of editing later. It's repetitive—you could sum it up in a few sentences. It looks like something that could be a compilation of messages Jeremiah delivered from time to time and has been put into some order. After Jeremiah redictated the scroll that the king burned, Jeremiah 36 also tells us that many other messages were added, to which my reaction is, "I bet they were!" And maybe that note implies some bits of editing and amplification of what Jeremiah dictated the first time, but my guess is that the chapters that follow (Jer 7–24) are the deposit of that ongoing process. It fits that at one level they are less organized than Jeremiah 2–6, but they have some headings that give them some structure, which I take to be the work of the curators. From time to time, the beginning of a chapter will say, "The word that came to Jeremiah from Yahweh," or something very similar. Those introductions lead into specific comments about things that Judah placed false trust in—not bad things, but things that Judah could look at the wrong way. So the outline of the first half of the scroll that follows isn't just something that I have thought up; it's based on features of the text. You'll find similar outlines in some other books on Jeremiah. But analyzing a book of the Bible is a bit like analyzing a painting or a piece of music— different people may analyze it in slightly different ways. Here's my version.

Introduction	1:1-19	
Part One	2:1–6:30	The scroll from 604
	2:1-37	Mostly confrontation
	3:1–4:4	Mostly exhortation to turn back
	4:5-31	Mostly warning
	5:1-31	Mostly confrontation
	6:1-30	Mostly (final) warning
Part Two	7:1–24:10	The additions from the next twenty years
	7:1–10:25	Exhortations and exchanges
	11:1–13:23	Jeremiah's arguments
	14:1–17:27	Drought, famine, sword
	18:1–20:18	Things come to a climax
	21:1–24:10	On kings and prophets
Conclusion	25:1-38	

On a formal level, this framework provides Jeremiah 1–25 with some structuring, but the same message keeps recurring through the different major sections—because Jeremiah had to keep giving the same message. The difference is more in the rhetoric than in the content—because Jeremiah had to try different ways of getting the same message home. But those sections do begin by seeking to undermine Judah's false trust:

- Jeremiah 2–6 begins by undermining assumptions about the exodus
- Jeremiah 7–10 begins by undermining assumptions about the temple
- Jeremiah 11–13 begins by undermining assumptions about Sinai
- Jeremiah 14–17 begins by undermining assumptions about prayer
- Jeremiah 18–20 begins by undermining assumptions about divine sovereignty
- Jeremiah 21–24 begins by undermining assumptions about David

Jeremiah 25 is then both the end of the first half of the scroll and the beginning of the second half, a kind of hinge, dated in the same year as the story in Jeremiah 36 about the first inscribing of a scroll.

JEREMIAH 25–52

The big difference between the first half of the scroll and the second half is that the first half comprises messages incorporating some stories, whereas the second half comprises stories incorporating some messages. The second half suggests another reason why the phrase "the book of Jeremiah" may be misleading. Not only do the reports of his messages not come neatly subject-by-subject. Although the scroll's introduction provides us with a chronological framework for Jeremiah's work, the scroll's stories don't come in chronological order. In Jeremiah 25–52, the main stories come in two complexes, and the main messages form a collection near the end.

Introduction	25:1–38	
Part Three	26:1–36:32	How disaster came to look inevitable but not final
	26:1–29:32	How people keep making the wrong decisions
	30:1–33:26	How God is nevertheless not finished
	34:1–36:32	How people keep making the wrong decisions
Part Four	37:1–45:5	How disaster came, and a new start was thrown away
	37:1–39:18	How disaster came
	40:1–44:30	How a new start was thrown away
	45:1-5	A footnote message for the scribe
Part Five	46:1–51:54	Messages about other nations
	46:1-28	Egypt
	47:1–49:39	Other nations, near and far
	50:1–51:64	Babylon
Coda	52:1-34	

Part three (Jer 26–36) is a compilation of separate stories and messages. The first and last stories relate to Jehoiakim's time; most of the others relate to Zedekiah's time. So they've been assembled into an organized sequence but not a chronological one. The sequence is more like a movie that jumps backwards and forwards in time, which keeps the audience on their toes and can clarify how different incidents relate to one other. Sometimes it helps to know the end and then see how things got there (as we will assume in the next chapter of this book, "Reading Jeremiah Backwards"). The gloom of the sequence is moderated by incorporating a compilation of God's promises, which (like most of Jeremiah's messages) don't have dates. Maybe they belong in the dark days when the fall of Jerusalem is about to happen or in the months and years that followed.

While part four (Jer 37–45) includes a little bit of going backwards as well as forwards, it is basically one continuous narrative, not a compilation. It's arguably more resolute in facing the stupid nature of the Judahite people and the dire consequences of their stupidity. There are no chapters full of promises here. On the other hand, it does close with a promise for Jeremiah's scribe, Baruch, who maybe stands for anyone who listens to Jeremiah, responds to his message, and encourages its preservation and sharing. The actual narrative ends with Jeremiah and Baruch in Egypt. Is that where the curators lived? Was Baruch among them? The questions link with a fact about the scroll that we have noted. Like the rest of the First Testament, it was eventually translated into Greek, and tradition says this translation was made in and for the flourishing Egyptian Jewish community in the time when Greek was the international language. Maybe (for instance) the scroll was compiled in Egypt and then taken to Judah or Babylon and expanded there, but also translated into Greek in Egypt.

Part five (Jer 46–51) broadens the scroll's horizon to cover Judah's neighbors, the big regional and world powers, and a couple of other sample far-off peoples. For the most part the messages about them talk of disaster, like the messages to Judah, though many incorporate promises of restoration and renewal, like the messages to Judah.

The entire scroll then closes (Jer 52) with a repeat of the account of the fall of Jerusalem and the aftermath, and finally with a report of the release of King Jehoiachin in Babylon in 562, which constitutes a little confirmation that Jeremiah's promises about Judah will ultimately come true.

CHAPTER TWO

READING JEREMIAH
BACKWARDS

:#:

In Jeremiah as in the Gospels, telling stories is a major way of doing theology. A difference is that the Gospels turned the individual stories about Jesus into one coherent story, whereas the stories in Jeremiah come in ones or in series but not in one sequence. It reflects the fact that Jesus is the real subject in the Gospels, whereas Jeremiah is not the real subject in the Jeremiah scroll. But we'll begin by trying to put the stories about Jeremiah together.

The Gospels tell the Jesus story in the logical way—birth to ministry to death to resurrection. Yet they know from the beginning where the story is going, and Jesus's entire story is told in light of his being on the way to death and resurrection. We'll look at the Jeremiah story on the basis of a similar insight, in the sense that we'll begin from the end and work backwards, as we look for the theology in the story.

JEREMIAH'S SIXTIETH OR SIXTY-FIFTH BIRTHDAY

In about the year 585 Jeremiah must have celebrated his sixtieth or sixty-fifth birthday. It was forty years since God commissioned him as a prophet to the nations, and he was in a foreign country, Egypt, a long way from home. Jeremiah 44 is the last we hear of him or from him, so maybe it would also have been his retirement celebration (priests did retire at sixty), though the chapter suggests it would not have been much of a celebration. We don't know when he died—the First Testament doesn't tell us about the death of any prophets except the ones who get lynched. His colleague, Baruch, who wrote down the scroll full of his messages in 604 that maybe lies behind Jeremiah 2–6, was with him in Egypt; perhaps Jeremiah spent a bit of time making sure that Baruch had a fuller reliable scroll with his messages in it for people to learn from. Baruch or someone else will also have compiled stories about Jeremiah and produced a first edition of a big scroll with a record of the messages and the stories. But that's a guess. All we know is that the last we hear of Jeremiah, he is living in Tanpanhes in the northeast region of Egypt. He is within striking distance of home, but he doesn't go back as far as we know.

He was there in the company of a community of people from Judah who had taken flight to Egypt a year or two previously. After the 587 catastrophe, they had settled in Mizpah, five miles north of Jerusalem, under the charge of one Gedaliah who had been appointed over the area by the Babylonians. But a man named Ishmael, with his allies, had assassinated Gedaliah, as well as some other Judahites in Mizpah and the Babylonian military garrison there. Ishmael presumably opposed the idea that Judah should simply submit to the rule of a Babylonian collaborator. Ishmael was a descendant of David who might reasonably have had aspirations to ruling Judah himself.

There were other Judahites who supported Gedaliah and his adminis-tration, and they set upon Ishmael, who deemed it wise to get out of Judah and take refuge across the Jordan in Ammon. Crisis over? Probably not. It would be a fair guess that the Babylonians would not be very interested in making subtle distinctions between one Judahite group and another, and that they would be sending a more impressive Babylonian military detail to make clear that you can't mess with the Babylonian-appointed administration in that way and expect to get away with it.

So this other company of Judahites hightailed it south to a country area near Bethlehem where nobody could find them and where they could decide what to do next. There they consulted Jeremiah and promised to do whatever Yahweh told him they should do. A week or so later, Jeremiah came back with the advice we might have expected—perhaps that was why he waited ten days until he was sure it was the right advice. They should sit tight and not be afraid of the Babylonians. Yahweh would look after them.

For all their promises, they behaved the same way as people usually did when Jeremiah gave them advice and did the opposite of what he said. In the

Bethlehem area, they were already near Judah's de facto southern border and on the road to Egypt. They decided to keep going in that direction. So that's how Jeremiah and Baruch ended up in Egypt. Maybe the others made Jeremiah and Baruch go with them, or maybe Jeremiah and Baruch knew they had to stay with them even if they were doing something stupid. One of the points about Jeremiah is that he represents God, and God often goes with people when they do the stupid thing.

If there's a similarity between the Jeremiah scroll and a Gospel, you could say that Jeremiah's story is like a Gospel without a resurrection story. It would be easy to imagine Jeremiah thinking that his life and ministry had been pointless. He had been a failure. But the very fact that we are reading the Jeremiah scroll now shows that it wasn't. You have no idea what God will do with your life or how God will bless people through you without your knowing it.

So that's how Jeremiah ended up in Egypt. But why was he in Mizpah?

Two Years Previously

It was July 587, and the Babylonian army had been laying siege to Jerusalem for two years. The Judahites had wanted to be in charge of their own destiny and had declared independence of Babylon; the Babylonians wanted to control the region so they could control the trade routes and make money, and had therefore marched southwest to put Jerusalem in its place. Two years is longer than it should have taken, but the army had to go off and sort out other business, which would have given Jerusalem a chance to replenish its provisions. But the army was now back and had been able to concentrate on this task, and Jerusalem had again run out of supplies.

It looks as if the Babylonians didn't have to break their way into the city. The Jerusalemites started to break their way out. The king, the rest of the administration, and the army knew they were doomed once the city fell. So they made a run for it, down into the Jordan Valley, maybe with the idea of disappearing across the Jordan into Moab or Ammon as Ishmael later did. But the Babylonians, who had been eating better and were probably fitter, caught up with them and captured the king, the person they really wanted, with his family and his staff. They took them off to Syria where the Babylonian king and commander-in-chief had his base, and there the king executed most of them. He made Zedekiah watch his sons being killed, then he blinded him and sent him off to Babylon, after which we hear nothing of him. The grim story is told twice in Jeremiah (Jer 39; 52), as well as in 2 Kings 25.

Meanwhile, Nebuzaradan, Nebuchadrezzar's lieutenant, was put in charge of things in Jerusalem. With relish he set about the devastation of the city, demolishing its walls and burning the temple, the palace, and the homes of ordinary people, making the city more or less uninhabitable, and taking off some of its remaining people to Babylon.

Initially, Jeremiah was among them. He had apparently been based in Jerusalem for some time. We don't know how he made a living, but he and his family had land in Anathoth, so maybe he got his support from there. But Jerusalem was where he delivered his messages, in the temple courtyard where people gathered and in the palace when summoned. But he would usually not have been welcome there because he spent much of his time haranguing the administration. And for some years he had been telling people that the Babylonians were actually Yahweh's agents in causing trouble to Jerusalem because, for various reasons, Yahweh had had it with Jerusalem.

Judah's official foreign policy was to ally with Egypt rather than submit to Babylon, though there might be people in Jerusalem who thought this policy was misguided and believed it would be more realistic to reaffirm allegiance to Babylon. Less than ten years previously, in 597, Nebuchadrezzar had paid an earlier visit to Judah, laid siege to the city, plundered the temple, and taken off to Babylon the then-king Jehoiachin and many other leading people—including Ezekiel, not a leading figure yet, but destined to be. Many people in Jerusalem and Judah would therefore have relatives and friends whom one could see as hostages in Babylon. In Judah there were certainly people who had personally gone over to the Babylonians, especially in parts of the country outside Jerusalem that were effectively under Babylonian control. And here is Jeremiah telling people that surrendering to Babylon is exactly what the city should do. He would look like someone in the pro-Babylonian rather than pro-Egyptian party, even though his argument was theological rather than political.

Perhaps it looked that way to the Babylonians themselves, who wouldn't care much about that subtle nuance. Jeremiah therefore didn't suffer the same fate as Jerusalem's official leadership but was put among the survivors of the siege and capture of the city who were being frog-marched to Babylon where they would do a useful job tending fields and working on other projects. Nebuzaradan had this company in a transit camp at Ramah, another town five miles north of Jerusalem, but there he gave Jeremiah various options. He could go to Babylon with the others. Or he could disappear into the Judahite countryside—the obvious move would be to go home to Anathoth. But there was a third possibility. Nebuchadrezzar had put a man called Gedaliah (the man we mentioned earlier in this chapter) in charge of Judah in its devastated state, with a base in Mizpah—another nearby small town.

There were several significant things about Gedaliah. His father Ahikam had played a role in rescuing Jeremiah when was he was in danger of being lynched (the story is in Jer 26). Ahikam and his father Shaphan had both been involved in encouraging the religious reformation in Judah during Josiah's reign, in the early years of Jeremiah's time as a prophet (the story is in 2 Kings 22). So Shaphan's family seems to have taken views more like Jeremiah's than like Zedekiah's. Maybe such considerations led to the Babylonians seeing Gedaliah as someone they could work with and led to Jeremiah's thinking the same for himself. So he chose to join Gedaliah's community at Mizpah, which became the de facto capital of Judah instead of the devastated Jerusalem. And that's how Jeremiah ended up in Egypt.

It's amazing how God keeps giving the people of God a new start and how we are capable of throwing it away. I picture God sitting with his cabinet in the heavens and they are all rolling their eyes at our stupidity and then starting another discussion about how they can fix things to give us another chance. But why did Jerusalem fall to the Babylonians?

TEN YEARS PREVIOUSLY

At one level the answer is: Zedekiah, the last ever descendant of David to reign as king in Jerusalem. The Jeremiah scroll lifts the veil on five moments in Zedekiah's reign; the Babylonians' own official records, the "Babylonian Chronicle," also give us some basic information about events in his time. Both sources are tantalizing. The Chronicle is tantalizing because it's just basic data, sometimes hard to read and understand, and patchy in the years that are covered by the bits of it that survive. On the other hand, the Jeremiah scroll doesn't relate the story in chronological order and it's not written like a history but with some imagination. So some imagination is also required in order to retell the story.

Zedekiah was never supposed to be king. It looks as if his eldest brother, Johanan, died young. His brothers Jehoahaz and Jehoiakim, and his nephew Jehoiachin, reigned ahead of him, but Jehoahaz got removed by the Egyptians, Jehoiakim died, and Jehoiachin got removed by the Babylonians. So the poisoned chalice fell to Zedekiah, courtesy of the Babylonians, who apparently thought he could be relied on to toe the line and not mess around courting the Egyptians.

They were wrong. Jerusalem had long been inclined to look to Egypt for support, and maybe Zedekiah was manipulated by pro-Egyptian forces in Jerusalem. Maybe Jerusalemites also took the view that the exiled Jehoiachin was the real king. It looks as if he had been the people's choice; Zedekiah was a Babylonian stooge. Another prophet told people in Jerusalem that God would soon be bringing Jehoiachin and the other exiles home (Jer 28; he was wrong).

We learn quite a bit about Zedekiah's tortuous relationship with Jeremiah, which maybe links with Zedekiah's doing poorly in the Jerusalem opinion polls. Jeremiah has long been telling people that Babylon is Yahweh's agent in bringing trouble to Judah as redress for its unfaithfulness to Yahweh. Paradoxically, perhaps, Judah's job was to submit to Babylonian authority. Submitting to the Babylonian club might even mean that Judah escaped from the Babylonian club. That's the message Jeremiah keeps giving Zedekiah, who is also therefore not very enthusiastic about Jeremiah.

Politically, things were quiet for the first three or four years of his reign, as far as we know. In about 594 Nebuchadrezzar had problems at home and abroad. The Babylonian Chronicle records that there was a rebellion in Babylon. It's maybe no coincidence that about this year, Jeremiah sent the Judahite exiles in Babylon a message to tell them to settle down and not to believe prophets who were telling them that they would soon be coming home (Jer 29). Nor is it a coincidence that in 594 envoys from Judah's neighbors to the east, Edom, Ammon, Moab, and from Tyre and Sidon to the northwest, were in Jerusalem, apparently trying to lean on Zedekiah to join in a show of independence from Babylon (Jer 27). Jeremiah went to see Zedekiah and told him, "Don't do it." The story doesn't say what happened then, but the Chronicle tells us that having sorted things out at home, Nebuchadrezzar took his army off on an expedition to the region, which was apparently a success; he came back with much plunder.

Eventually, in 589, Zedekiah did rebel, as the independence advocates said, and Nebuchadrezzar duly arrived in Judah. In keeping with usual and logical practice, first he dealt with the rest of the country—the rural areas with their unfortified towns and villages, and the big towns of Lachish and Azekah. Then he blockaded Jerusalem. Zedekiah put Jeremiah under house arrest (Jer 32); obviously his preaching about submission to Babylon would undermine Zedekiah's policies. But the house arrest meant he lived in the palace environs, and from time to time Zedekiah would consult him, or Jeremiah would take the initiative in going to see Zedekiah. Zedekiah cannot escape defeat, capture, and exile by Nebuchadrezzar, Jeremiah would tell him, but by surrendering he can escape death and die in peace (Jer 34).

In 588 the siege was relieved for a while when Nebuchadrezzar's army went to look after that business elsewhere, and Zedekiah sent people to ask Jeremiah to pray for them or to ask what was going to happen now. They'll be back, he was able to tell Zedekiah—not on the basis of his political acumen but because he knew what Yahweh was doing. He himself left the city to visit his home village to sort something out in connection with the family land there (Jer 37), and not unreasonably the city guard thought he was defecting to the Babylonians, arrested him, and got him put in jail. There Zedekiah consulted him again and, understandably in the circumstances, got a dusty reply. But Jeremiah did prevail over him simply to be put back under house arrest. Some other leading figures in Jerusalem were not so amenable and wanted to silence Jeremiah once and for all, but an African member of the palace staff discovered what was going on and got the king again to see that Jeremiah was rescued. In that same context, there's an intriguing story about Zedekiah and the more well-to-do people in Jerusalem and their bondservants (Jer 34). The well-to-do were not releasing their bondservants after six years of service, as the Torah required. In the context of the siege, they started doing it, maybe because in a siege, servants were more of a liability than an asset. Then the siege ceased when Nebuchadrezzar's army left, and the Jerusalem householders abandoned their policy to release their bondservants. It led to Jeremiah warning them that disaster would follow. Nebuchadrezzar would be back. And he was. So that's how Jerusalem fell and Zedekiah met his terrible fate.

There's a story about a man who fell over a cliff but managed to grab hold of a tree branch to stop him falling to his death. He called out, hoping to attract the attention of someone who could help him: "Is there anyone there?" A voice came from the heavens: "Let go and I'll catch you." The man thought for a moment and eventually called out, "Is there anyone else there?" Through the decade of Zedekiah's reign, Jeremiah gave people one crazy option: surrender to the Babylonians and things will work out. Most people never believed him. But it's never over until it's over, and God kept giving another chance to the city, its people, and its king. But they resolutely refused their chances, and eventually it was over—at least, it was for Jerusalem and for Zedekiah.

What set this sequence of events going? Why did Nebuchadrezzar want to control Jerusalem? And why did Jeremiah say it was going to happen? For the answer to these questions we need once more to look back.

THE WORD OF GOD AT THE CRITICAL MOMENT

Zedekiah's brother Jehoiakim reigned from 609 to 597. So the fourth year of his reign was 604. It was the year when things began to catch up with Judah, and when the Babylonians (and God) began to catch up with Jehoiakim. He had been put on the throne by the Egyptians as their puppet, but the Egyptians had just suffered a humiliating defeat at the hands of the Babylonians. It was one of the first triumphs of the great Nebuchadrezzar, the prelude to his becoming king of Babylon in succession to his father Nabopolassar. 604 was a year like 1812 or 1914 or 1939. Anyone who could read the newspapers could see which way the wind was blowing.

It was in this year that Jeremiah sensed that Yahweh was telling him to have one last attempt to persuade Judah to turn back. He was to write down the prophecies he had delivered over the twenty-three years of his ministry. It meant producing what may have been in effect the first edition of the Jeremiah scroll. He had long been telling people they must turn to Yahweh or be cast off, and they had been ignoring him, or rather laughing at him, because the disaster didn't come. For them, and at times for Jeremiah himself, it seemed to indicate that Jeremiah's word couldn't be believed. It never came true.

Jeremiah's feelings as he received this commission may therefore have included a sense of relief that the critical moment had at last arrived. The political situation finally seemed to be proving that he was right. Yahweh was at last acting in accordance with his word. So Jeremiah summoned his colleague Baruch. Baruch could write, so he could take Jeremiah's words down; perhaps Jeremiah couldn't write. But also Baruch was free to visit the temple. Everyone used to go there to rejoice at festivals and to pray on fast days, but Jeremiah couldn't; perhaps the authorities got weary of him causing trouble by telling everyone that the king and the priests were ignoring God's words to them and had banned him.

Baruch was just as committed to Yahweh as Jeremiah was, though this commitment didn't make identifying himself with Jeremiah easy; he had seen how people had been treating Jeremiah. He had seen the price Jeremiah paid for being a prophet. He knew that in a situation like theirs, declaring Yahweh's word cost you something. A natural feeling of being scared stiff and a conviction about the trustworthiness of Jeremiah's God coexisted in his heart.

They set about the task of putting Jeremiah's prophecies into writing. Some months elapsed until the right occasion presented itself. Nebuchadrezzar's army marched down the west coast of Judah, past where Tel Aviv is now, and attacked and sacked the Philistine port of Ashkelon. The Babylonians were breathing down Jehoiakim's neck. That same month people assembled in Jerusalem to fast and pray. This occasion was the moment that Baruch took the scroll to the temple court, the area where people wandered about and talked in the way we read about in the Gospels. He gathered people around him and began to read Jeremiah's warnings about the Babylonians bringing death and desolation to the land. People on the temple staff heard about it and someone decided they'd better tell the state authorities, who sent for Baruch.

They cross-examined him and discovered how Jeremiah had gotten around the ban on his public appearances. They were presumably frustrated that their plans to silence him had failed, and they knew they had to tell the king what was going on. But they also knew that once they took that action, they had signed Jeremiah and Baruch's death warrant. So they warned Baruch that the two of them had better disappear. It perhaps proves that they didn't feel very loyal to Jehoiakim, the king who had been foisted on them by the Egyptians. It also hints that in their heart of hearts they knew Jeremiah was right. They had gone away from Yahweh. They were still present in the temple, but spiritually and morally they were miles away from him. Baruch had caught them off-guard with the word of God. They proved themselves to be the spiritual sons of the officials in Josiah's day who knew how to respond to the scroll read in the temple on that occasion (see 2 Kings 22).

But they confiscated the scroll and reported to the king what had happened. He sent for the scroll and got a member of his staff called Jehudi to read it out loud. It was December and evidently cold in Jerusalem, as it can be (it snows sometimes). Jehoiakim was in his winter quarters and had a fire going. Jehudi read systematically through the scroll, column by column. But the king didn't let him wind the scroll onto the equivalent of a take-up reel. Each time he had finished three or four columns the king would reach out and hack it off, so that the scroll dropped section by section into the flames of the fire.

Perhaps it was partly an act of bravado on Jehoiakim's part, designed to show that it took more than a prophet and his tin-pot assistant to put King Jehoiakim off. But there would have been more to it. The situation was worse now that Jeremiah had put all those words into writing. Spoken words are all very well, but they can be lost in the wind; a person can't necessarily be held to them. Putting things into writing makes them definite and fixed. All the more so with putting things into writing in the name of God. Even a king who liked to think of himself as a cool and worldly-wise politician would have found it a bit scary to have there in writing God's declared intention to bring disaster upon him. Jehoiakim's act was designed to stop Jeremiah's words from coming true by destroying them.

Of course, it was naive to think that he could frustrate God's purpose by burning his words. In any case, it was only too easy for Jeremiah and Baruch to start again, perhaps looking after the scroll better this time. Jeremiah knew that Jehoiakim had crossed a line. He had gone too far. The wimps on his staff had been caught unaware by God's word and had let themselves be convicted by it. The king wasn't going to let himself be tricked, or exhorted, or reasoned into a change of policy. He was too far gone. He would rather rip the scroll than rip his clothes. Whereas his father Josiah knew how to respond to the word of Yahweh, Jehoiakim did not.

It's a story full of suggestiveness about the word of God:

- about the risks some people took to deliver the words that we now have in the Scriptures
- about God's faithfulness to people who declare his word faithfully
- about how much of the Scriptures are warnings hanging over the people of God
- about how God's word can sometimes get through to people when their defenses are down, when they are unprepared to be hit by it
- about how scary it is that we have God's word in writing and about how taking that for granted is as effective as burning it
- about how dangerous it can be to ignore God's word
- about how you cannot destroy God's word, silence it, drown it, or ban it; it will keep resurfacing

BEFORE THE TRAGEDY

Half a century before, the king of Judah had been Jehoiakim's great-grand-father, Manasseh. He had ruled for half a century and Judah had been doing well. They were under the distant control of the Assyrians, but as long as they kept their heads down and paid their taxes, they could get on with their lives.

But there's a hint that part of keeping their heads down was assimilating the state's official faith to the faith of the Assyrians. Religion can hold an empire together. And it had always been the case that ordinary people were attached to the traditional religion of Canaan as well as to the faith of Israel. One of the traits of this religion that most offended Jeremiah was being willing to offer your child as a sacrifice to a god as a way of showing how committed you were.

After Manasseh came his son Amon, but he was assassinated after two years and his eight-year-old son, Josiah, was put on the throne. There were some faceless and nameless people actually running things. The Assyrian empire was beginning to decline, which opened up the possibility of both political and religious independence for Judah. So a religious reformation started, which Josiah backed with enthusiasm as he grew up. Second Kings 22 tells a great story about how the senior priest Hilkiah found a Torah scroll in the temple during its remodeling. Reactions to it were the opposite of the king's reactions narrated in Jeremiah 36. Like that scroll of Jeremiah's messages, this scroll warned people of the consequences that would follow if they ignored it. Josiah (now twenty-eight) made it the basis for a thoroughgoing reformation in Judah. The reactions people showed and the actions Josiah took overlap with Deuteronomy, so maybe the scroll was a version of what we know as Deuteronomy. The discovery happened four years after God commissioned Jeremiah as a prophet, and Jeremiah's references to Josiah in Jeremiah 3 and Jeremiah 21 suggest he was enthusiastic about it, but it's a matter of guesswork which of Jeremiah's prophesies might come from that period.

So far so good. But a decade or so later, Josiah made a fatal mistake. As Assyria (in the north of modern Iraq) declined, Babylonia (to the south in Iraq) and Media (in modern Iran) positioned themselves to take over the empire. Egypt was keen to support the old order so that it could carry on being the major power in its own region and prepared to join Assyria in battle against Babylonia and Media. Josiah thought it was in Judah's interests for Assyria to fall, and he tried to intervene. But the Egyptian army brushed Judah off like a fly, and Josiah got killed.

His son Jehoahaz succeeded him, but the Egyptians deposed him, which is how his brother Jehoiakim came to be on the throne. Presumably the Egyptians thought their appointee would be more likely to follow policies they approved, and in the short term it worked: Jehoiakim made sure that Judah paid the fine that the Egyptians imposed on Judah for their effrontery in attacking their army. But the Egyptians had been right that it was not in their interests for Babylon to become the major power in the Middle East. Having taken over from Assyria, the Babylonians were soon interested in asserting authority over the Mediterranean countries because of the importance of the trade routes to the Mediterranean and Arabia, and Judah became part of the area they controlled.

To Jeremiah, that development would be the least problematic aspect of Jehoiakim's reign—indeed, maybe it was not problematic at all. He might have taken the view that Josiah's meddling with Egypt was not merely a political and military mistake but a religious and theological one. Jeremiah shows no theological or religious interest in Judah being involved with other nations politically or militarily. Let God look after those issues.

Judging from Jeremiah 36 and many of Jeremiah's messages, it looks as if Jehoiakim had abandoned the principles and practice of his father's reformation. Things were back to the way they had been in his great-grandfather's day. Josiah's reformation turned out to have been superficial in its effects. It went against the instincts of ordinary people. It was as if the wrongdoing of Manasseh and all the innocent blood he had shed had a continuing and fatal effect on Judah. It's not exactly that God makes one generation suffer for the sins of previous generations, though 2 Kings 24 comes close to that explanation. It's that the wrongdoing of one generation does have an effect on following generations. It may require a miracle to halt that process.

CHAPTER THREE

THE THEMES IN
JEREMIAH 1-25

W E ' V E S E E N T H A T O N E W A Y of looking at the structure of the Jeremiah
scroll is to see it as taking up facets of First Testament faith on which Israel
needs to get its thinking and its commitments straight. In this chapter, we
start from the way in which aspects of that faith form the jumping-off point
for different sections of the scroll, sometimes making the discussion of a
theme a basis for looking at the way that theme appears elsewhere in the scroll.

JEREMIAH 2-6 BEGINS: THINK ABOUT THE EXODUS

Jeremiah 2-6 (perhaps a slightly expanded version of the first scroll that Jeremiah dictated) opens by recalling Israel's exodus from Egypt and its journey
through the wilderness.

> I have kept in mind for you the commitment of your youth,
>   your love as a bride,
> Your going after me through the wilderness,
>   through a country not sown.
> Israel was sacred to Yahweh,
>   the first fruits of his yield.
> All the people who ate of it would incur liability;
>   bad fortune would come upon them. . . .

What did your ancestors find that was evil in me,
    that they went far away from me,
Went after something hollow and became hollow,
    and didn't say "Where is Yahweh,
The one who got us up from the country of Egypt
    and enabled us to go through the wilderness,
Through a country of steppe and pit,
    through a country of drought and deep darkness,
Through a country through which no one passed
    and where no human being lived?" (Jer 2:2-3, 5-6)

Maybe it's no coincidence that Jeremiah's summary of his message begins with the exodus, which was, after all, the beginning of Israel's story as a people. To be more precise, his summary starts with Israel's time in the wilderness, its journey from Egypt to the promised land, though eventually it comes to the exodus itself. The beginning of Israel's story was Yahweh's getting Israel out of Egypt and up to Canaan—"up," because Egypt is low-lying, while Israel's heartland is mountain country. The exodus was an amazing act of deliverance to be followed by equally amazing provision as the people passed through the tough landscape between Egypt and Canaan, through a country not sown— little of it gets enough rainfall to make sowing realistic.

Israel was Yahweh's young bride, and he made sure of looking after his bride. The relationship was not like a Western egalitarian marriage but a patriarchal one, which didn't mean it was despotic but did mean that the "husband" was the authority figure, the protector, and the provider. Israel's responsibility was simply to be faithful to the relationship like a wife to a husband. It meant trusting him to be her protector and provider, and Yahweh remembered Israel's commitment and loyalty in those early days. "Commitment" is *hesed*, often translated "steadfast love." It suggests resolute and unwavering faithfulness. "Love" is *ahabah*, which is also usually translated "love," and also suggests a love that expresses itself in loyalty and commitment ("if you love me, keep my commandments"; Jn 14:15).

Reading the story in Exodus through Deuteronomy may make you ask whether Yahweh is looking back to the beginnings of this marriage with rose-tinted spectacles, but there is a contrast between Israel's commitment to him after the exodus and what's happened since. Back then, they were in awe of Yahweh and they trusted in Yahweh. Not so much now. Then, they "went after" him, followed him. More recently they "went after" something hollow, went after the empty gods that other people in Canaan followed and looked to as protectors and providers.

Why haven't they been asking where is the God who got them up from Egypt? His provision on their way from Egypt to Canaan included making sure that they had enough to eat and protecting them from attack, which continue to be Israel's needs once they have reached Canaan. But Israel gives up on looking to the God of the exodus to meet these needs. They look to the traditional gods of Canaan to make the crops grow, perhaps on the basis that they *are* the gods of Canaan. It's their territory. They can deliver. And Israel looks to people like Assyria and Egypt for political and military help. Given the country where the exodus took them from, looking to the Egyptians is ironic.

When things are difficult, the implication is that you ask where God is and that the exodus is your model for the way you expect God to relate to you. Israel didn't think that way. They had forgotten about the exodus, that key event at the beginning of their story. They had been living as serfs there and Yahweh had got them out. Why aren't they looking to that God now?

Fortunately, Yahweh hasn't forgotten. Later, when the disaster of 587 is about to happen or has happened, he himself will again recall the exodus and that journey through the wilderness.

> The people found grace in the wilderness,
>   those who survived the sword.
> As Israel went to find its rest,
>   "From afar Yahweh appeared to me."
> With permanent love I loved you;
>   therefore I've drawn you out with commitment. (Jer 31:2-3)

There is "love" again, but here it is referring to Yahweh's love or loyalty. In 587 you might not have thought that Yahweh's loyalty or love was permanent, so Yahweh declares that they are. The catastrophe of 587 will not be the end of the relationship. Adding a new reference to "commitment" (again Yahweh's commitment, not theirs) underlines the point. The very nature of commitment is that it keeps going even when the other party forfeits any right to it. Further, here Yahweh actually begins by reminding Israel that it found "grace" (*hen*) in the wilderness. Grace is the action that sets commitment going in the first place. You can only "find" grace. You can't earn it. Which is just as well, because Israel hasn't even tried. Sometimes Christian readers think that Israel's relation with God was based on law, not on grace. Not so. By God's grace Israel survived Pharaoh's sword, were on their way to find their rest in the promised land, and could testify that "from afar Yahweh appeared to me." Now Yahweh can say, "I haven't changed." Now will they ask in their situation of need, "Where is Yahweh"?

In the next chapter of the scroll, on the eve of the fall of Jerusalem, and therefore perhaps at about the same time as Yahweh gave Israel that reminder of his love and commitment, Jeremiah reminds Yahweh and reminds himself about some of those facts about Yahweh's relationship with Israel. Yahweh has just given him instructions to claim ownership of some land in Anathoth, on behalf of his family. It will involve shelling out some money. It looks like an insane idea. Jeremiah knows better than anyone that the city is about to fall and that land values in the region are plummeting. But he sets the process going, reminding Yahweh and himself that "nothing is too extraordinary for you" (Jer 32:17), the one

> who put down signs and portents in the country of Egypt to this day, and in Israel and among humanity, and made a name for yourself this very day. You got your people Israel out of the country of Egypt with signs and portents and with a strong hand and a bent arm and with great fearfulness. You gave them this country that you swore to their ancestors to give them, a country flowing with milk and syrup. They came and possessed it. (Jer 32:20-23)

In response, Yahweh nicely asks Jeremiah whether he really thinks there is nothing too extraordinary for him to do (Jer 32:27). The word *extraordinary* recurs in the exodus story: the exodus involved Yahweh doing "extraordinary" things (Ex 3:20; 15:11). The exodus story and its aftermath show that Yahweh could get his people out of serfdom and give them a land to live on. So he could do it again. Jeremiah has put his money where his mouth is, and things will work out. There is a stock market principle of buying low in order to sell high (that is, you buy stocks that people don't think are very valuable in the conviction that they will go up in price). Yahweh will make it work for Jeremiah. Not that he will actually ever sell it, though neither does he go to live on the land when he has the chance (as we saw in "Two Years Previously" in chap. 2).

Jeremiah 2–6 as a whole unfolds as follows:

2:1-37	mostly a confrontation of Judah for seeking the everyday help of the traditional gods of Canaan and the political help of Egypt—for which it has been paying a penalty already

3:1–4:4	mostly an exhortation to Judah to turn back to Yahweh, learning a lesson from the fate of northern Israel (Ephraim) which had been invaded by Assyria
4:5-31	mostly a warning about devastation that will also come to Judah (here and elsewhere, Jeremiah can describe things as happening now when they are actually future)
5:1-31	mostly a confrontation that additionally condemns people's unfaithfulness to one another and their failure to protect the powerless and needy
6:1-30	mostly a warning about devastation by an unnamed northern invader, with a conclusion that Yahweh has tested and rejected the people

JEREMIAH 7–10 BEGINS: THINK ABOUT THE TEMPLE

Jeremiah 7–10 begins with Yahweh commissioning Jeremiah to urge people to think about the temple and about their life and about the relationship between them.

Stand at the gateway of Yahweh's house and call out this word there. You're to say, "Listen to Yahweh's word, all of Judah who are coming through these gateways to bow low to Yahweh. Yahweh of Armies, Israel's God, has said this: 'Make your ways and your practices good, and I'll let you dwell in this place. Don't rely for yourselves on words of falsehood: "These buildings are Yahweh's palace, Yahweh's palace, Yahweh's palace." Rather, make your ways and your practices truly good. If you really exercise authority between an individual and his neighbour, don't exploit alien, orphan, and widow, don't shed the blood of someone who is free of guilt in this place, and don't follow other gods with bad results for yourselves, I'll let you dwell in this place, in the country that I gave to your ancestors from of old, permanently.

There, you're relying for yourselves on words of falsehood that won't prevail. Is there stealing, murder, adultery, swearing falsely, and burning sacrifices to the Master, and following other gods that you didn't acknowledge, and you come and stand before me in this house over which my name has been called out and say "We are rescued"—in order to do all these offensive things? Has it become a cave for thugs in your eyes, this house over which my name has been called out? Yes, I myself, I've been looking (Yahweh's declaration).

Because you can go to my site that was at Shiloh where I let my name dwell before, and look at what I did to it in the face of my people Israel's bad dealing. So now because of your doing all these things (Yahweh's declaration), and I've spoken to you, speaking assiduously, but you haven't listened, and I've called you but you haven't answered, I shall do to the house over which my name has been called out, on which you're relying, the site that I gave to you and your ancestors, as I did to Shiloh.'" (Jer 7:1-14)

We have noted that the temple courtyard was an obvious place for Jeremiah to preach if he wanted to reach people. Jesus too sometimes talks about the temple when he preaches there, and on one occasion refers to this very story (Mk 11:15-19). When Jeremiah or Jesus talk about it on these two occasions, the problem they confront is not that people have forgotten about the temple as they have forgotten about the exodus. It's that they have lost track of its significance.

Hebrew doesn't have a word equivalent to *temple* in the sense of an impressive sacred building. When English Bibles have the word *temple*, they are translating words that mean either "house" or "palace." Israel has lost track of the significance of the temple as being "Yahweh's house" or "Yahweh's palace." While his main house or palace is in the heavens, the temple is the place he chose to have as a second home, when David suggested it. He let Israel build it for him and promised to meet with them there. It's thus a building over which his name has been proclaimed—in other words, he owns it. It's not just an ordinary house; it can indeed be called his palace because it is a splendid building and because he is the king, the commander-in-chief of the universe, "Yahweh of Armies."

Israel behaves as if it has lost track of the significance of this palace. One aspect of its lapse relates to the community commitments that are important to this king, which are one aspect of the expectations expressed in the Ten Commandments. They involve seeing that relationships between neighbors work out in a fair way, that Israelites don't exploit people who are vulnerable because they don't have land or have lost their land—foreigners, orphans, widows, and innocent people who can be deprived of their land on trumped up charges. Jeremiah 2–6 has also made clear that Israel has lost track of the religious commitments that are important to Yahweh. There were various aspects to this failure—maybe they affected different people at different times. There was the inclination to offer sacrifices to other gods at other shrines as well as praying to Yahweh in the temple. Yahweh here refers more specifically to the object of that worship. Translations usually call him Ba'al, but that word is Hebrew for lord and master, so I translate his name "the Master." It's the natural way for Canaanites to think of him, but not Israelites. Later in this section, Jeremiah will speak of people relating to Yahweh in a way he hated, of which sacrificing a child was the most abhorrent.

Jeremiah also spells out what worship actually means. Hebrew doesn't have an all-purpose word equivalent to the English word *worship*, but Yahweh usefully spells out the nature of worship in a series of verbs when he speaks of the gods the people loved, served, went after, inquired of, and bowed low to (Jer 8:2). They were worshiping but in the wrong direction. To put it positively, the worship that Yahweh looks for means giving him the loyal love that he referred to earlier (Jer 2:2), serving him by bringing him your offerings, going after him as your guide, leader, and commander, inquiring of him about problems and issues, and bowing low to him so that you worship him with your body and not just your mind and heart.

But at the moment, even perfectly good acts of worship are abhorrent to him:

> What use to me is incense that comes from Sheba,
> or fine cane from a far-off country?
> Your burnt offerings don't find acceptance,
> your sacrifices aren't pleasing to me. (Jer 6:20)

Yahweh declares rhetorically or hyperbolically that worship wasn't the thing he gave any instructions about when he brought Israel out of Egypt (Jer 7:21-23). What he wanted was that people should listen to him and do the kinds of things the Ten Commandments say. Prayer meetings, festivals of praise: they mean nothing when Israel is behaving as if the temple were the kind of cave where thugs could hide. There is a double irony about that image—you can't hide from Yahweh, especially in his own house!

It's not the first time the Israelites have made the mistake they're making. When they arrived in Canaan, they set up Yahweh's dwelling in Shiloh, twenty miles north of Jerusalem. That shrine was the first place over which Yahweh's name was proclaimed, or (as Yahweh puts it here) the place where he let his name dwell (Jer 7:12). It wasn't just that they called it Yahweh's house. He collaborated with their doing so. He was quite willing to be associated with it. He settled his name there. And the name stands for the person: when people proclaimed the name of Yahweh and called on Yahweh by name, it reminded them that the God with that name was there. He himself treated it as his second home. But in due course Yahweh let that Shiloh dwelling be destroyed. If he could do it once, he could do it again. The mere fact that this building is Yahweh's palace is not something to be relied on, something to keep going on about ("these buildings are Yahweh's palace, Yahweh's palace, Yahweh's palace"). There are other facts you need to attend to.

Jeremiah 7–10 unfolds as follows:

7:1–8:3	exhortations, confrontations, and warnings about worship:
	worship not accompanied by faithfulness to one another (Jer 7:1-15)
	worship of the Queen of the Heavens, a supreme goddess (Jer 7:16-20)
	worship not accompanied by a life that follows what Yahweh says (Jer 7:21-28)
	worship that involves sacrificing a son or daughter to Yahweh (Jer 7:29-34)
	worship that involves looking to the sun, moon, and stars (Jer 8:1-3)
8:4–9:26	three exchanges between Yahweh, Judah, and Jeremiah:
	Yahweh challenges Judah about not turning and about the falseness of scribes, priests, and prophets; and Judah expresses its sense of panic and anguish (Jer 8:4-20)
	Jeremiah laments at Judah's suffering; and Yahweh responds by pointing out why he needs to take action against Judah (Jer 8:21–9:16)
	Yahweh or Jeremiah bids Judah to do the sensible thing and commission its mourners; and Yahweh issues a reminder about true smartness and true circumcision (Jer 9:17-26)
10:1-25	another exhortation and another exchange, implying the context of the first exile in 597
	a return to exhortation about worship—here to warn people about the stupidity of images as used by the Babylonians as an aid to worship (see the "Other Faiths" in chap. 5 below) (Jer 10:1-16)
	another exchange between Yahweh, Jeremiah, and Judah—here Jeremiah speaks to Jerusalem and for Jerusalem in light of the prospect of further exile (Jer 10:17-25)

JEREMIAH 11–13 BEGINS: THINK ABOUT THE COVENANT

Jeremiah 11–13 begins by talking about the "covenant" between Yahweh and Israel. The Hebrew word for covenant is *berit*, but that word can also mean treaty, contract, pledge, obligation, or bond—any solemnly undertaken commitment that one party makes to another or that two parties make to each other. In turn, the English word *covenant* has its own range of meanings that overlaps with the Hebrew word but isn't the same: we may think that covenants must be mutual or that equality is of the essence of a covenantal relationship, but neither mutuality nor equality need apply to a *berit*. Outside Jeremiah 11, Jeremiah doesn't use the word *berit* very often to describe the relationship between Yahweh and Israel (most of the other references come in Jeremiah 31–34). On the other hand, in passages such as Jeremiah 2:5-8 and Jeremiah 7:22-23 he was talking about a covenantal relationship (in our terms) even though he didn't use the word *berit*.

To discourage us from reading our ideas of covenant into Jeremiah, I'll use the English word *pledge* when he uses the word *berit*. So Yahweh made a pledge to the Israelites when he got them out of Egypt and required them also to solemnize it. The pledge meant their listening to what he said and acting on it.

"The person is cursed who doesn't listen to the words in this pledge that I ordered your ancestors on the day I got them out from the country of Egypt, from the iron smelter, saying 'Listen to my voice and act on them in accordance with all that I order you, and you will be a people for me and I will be God for you,' in order to implement the oath that he swore to your ancestors to give them a country flowing with milk and syrup this very day."

I said, "Yes, Yahweh."

And Yahweh said to me, "Call out all these words in Judah's towns and in Jerusalem's streets: 'Listen to the words in this pledge and act on them. Because I testified solemnly to your ancestors on the day I got them out from the country of Egypt and until this day, testifying assiduously, saying "Listen to my voice." But they didn't listen or bend their ear but walked each person by the bad determination of their mind. So I brought on them all the words in this pledge that I ordered them to act on but they didn't act on.'"

Yahweh said to me, "A conspiracy can be found among Judah's people and among Jerusalem's inhabitants. They've turned back to the wayward acts of their ancestors of old, who refused to listen to my words. As those people followed other gods, Israel's household and Judah's household have contravened my pledge that I solemnized with their ancestors." (Jer 11:3-10)

The covenant or pledge is something Yahweh commanded. He imposed it on Israel. He was like a big power such as Assyria imposing the terms of a relationship on a little power such as Judah. Therein lies some of the background to Jeremiah's speaking in terms of a *berit*, a treaty or covenant between Yahweh and Israel. It's not that Yahweh is simply a dictator. There are two sides to the relationship, as there were between Assyria and Judah. Judah benefited from the relationship in return for surrendering its independence.

Israel first benefited because Yahweh got them out of Egypt. Why did he need to do so? Egypt is a nice place (Brits go there for winter holidays), but in Israel's day it was nice only for Egyptians. For iron ore to become usable, it has to be heated to a horrifically high temperature, to melt out the slag and thus produce pure metal. For Israelites, life in Egypt was life in an iron smelter. Yahweh later describes it as life in a household of serfs or slaves (Jer 34:13).

Israel benefitted again because Yahweh took them into Canaan, a country with so much land for sheep and goats it seemed to be flowing with milk, and so much land for orchards it seemed to be flowing with the syrup that was to be made from the fruit of the trees (traditionally, translations speak of the land flowing with honey, but fruit syrup is the sweetness the word usually denotes).

On the basis of those acts of liberation and generosity and of Israel's response, Yahweh could say that they would be his people and he would be their God. He would lay before them the kind of life he expected from them in response to his generosity, and they would live it, and he would continue his blessing, and so on forever. Such was the promise he made, the oath he swore. But the other side of his oath was the curse that hung over people if they didn't keep their side of the commitment. Ignore the expectations of the pledge and you get into a lot of trouble. Judah knew from experience that it was true, in its relationship with Assyria or Babylon and with Yahweh.

In light of the way the pledge worked, it might be misleading to say that Yahweh was liberating Israel from Egypt. He wasn't granting them their freedom, and Jeremiah doesn't talk in those terms. As would be the case when Jesus died in order to get people out of servitude, Yahweh was actually removing them from service to one master so that they entered the service of another master. If this relationship was to work, they had to listen to his voice; "listen" (*shama*) denotes listening that issues in obedience. When one enters into this pledged relationship, one makes up one's mind to give up making up one's own mind about some basic things. But "they didn't listen or bend their ear but walked each person by the bad determination of their mind"; that phrase recurs in Jeremiah's critique of Judah (Jer 3:17; 7:24; 9:14; 11:8; 13:10; 16:12; 18:12; 23:17).

Long ago, both parties to this pledge had "solemnized" it; Yahweh later refers to his "solemnizing" when he speaks of having got them out of a serf household (Jer 34:13). Literally, they had "cut" the pledge (*karat*). Making a pledge could involve cutting an animal in two and walking between its parts, with an explicit or implicit prayer that you may be torn apart like the animal if you fail to keep your word. Yahweh refers to this aspect of pledge-making (Jer 34:18-20). It wasn't the first time he had made this pledge. Genesis 15:7-20 provides an eye-popping account of the first time. It means that he *had* to rescue the Israelites from Egypt and bring them to Canaan because he had made a promise to their ancestors. He here uses the term *ancestors* in two different connections. The present generation's nearer ancestors were the people Yahweh got out of Egypt. But the people he made his promise to were these ancestors' ancestors. He names them just once in the Jeremiah scroll as Abraham, Isaac, and Jacob (Jer 33:26).

Jeremiah himself once refers to this promise that Yahweh "swore" (Jer 32:22). The scroll does on other occasions refer to Yahweh swearing to do something, but it is something negative (Jer 22:13; 44:26; 49:13; 51:14). One would surely expect Yahweh's yes to mean yes and his no to mean no (cf. Mt 5:37), but speaking in terms of an oath indicates for his people how seriously he made this undertaking. Yahweh accommodated himself to Israel by undertaking this act of swearing, to underwrite his commitment, as he did in swearing that he would keep his promise despite the fact that for him more than for anyone yes would be yes and no would be no. Yahweh's willingness to accommodate himself to his people in this way is a marked expression of his love.

It is because Israel has failed to keep its side of the pledge that it has become a people "cursed" by the sanction it wished on itself when it made the pledge. Yahweh's references to the curse and the pledge, and to his becoming God for the people and Israel's becoming a people for him, exposes the trickiness involved in discussing the interrelationship between the two parties' mutual commitment. Was Yahweh's pledge conditional? We talk about love being unconditional. But putting the question this way causes more problems than it solves (as it does in human relationships). Yahweh's grace and commitment were not conditional, but they did require a response of commitment, otherwise the relationship wouldn't work. Or we could say that Yahweh's promises were unconditioned but they were conditional. The reason Yahweh made his promises to Israel's ancestors and got them out of Egypt into their new country wasn't something they did that commended them to Yahweh. But his acts of deliverance and blessing required a response on their part, and it was the shortfall in that response that led to the destruction of Jerusalem. Likewise, when Yahweh promises that he will restore Israel, he does not imply that it will be Israel's turning back to him that will result in the restoration of Israel. He will again do it because he has made a pledge. But Jeremiah does indicate the anticipation of Israel to live by Yahweh's expectations as a result of his act of restoration. And if one were to ask what will happen if Israel fails to, then one might expect Jeremiah to respond in the same way as Paul does in relation to the equivalent question in Romans 6. Paul's argument there fits the ambiguity in Jeremiah and points out further the disadvantages in the language of conditional/unconditional.

Yes, Yahweh's grace issues from him, not from his people's deservingness. But yes, his people's commitment is absolutely required as a response to that grace. And if you question whether God will turn away from you if you don't keep your commitment, you have missed the point.

Jeremiah 11–13 as a whole unfolds as follows:

11:1-17	a message about the pledge
	a confrontation and the warning (Jer 11:1-13)
	an instruction not to pray for Jerusalem (Jer 11:14-17)
11:18–12:17	three exchanges between Jeremiah and Yahweh
	Jeremiah's protest: I was like a lamb led to the slaughter (Jer 11:18-20)
	Yahweh's response: I will attend to them (Jer 11:21-23)
	Jeremiah's protest: why are people who betray me doing well? (Jer 12:1-4)
	Yahweh's response: things are going to get worse; deal with it (Jer 12:5-6)
	Yahweh's protest: what about the fact that I abandoned my house? (Jer 12:7-13)
	Yahweh's response to himself: I will again have compassion (Jer 12:14-17)
13:1-27	five more warnings
	a story about name, praise, and splendor (Jer 13:1-12a)
	a metaphor conveying a threat of devastation (Jer 13:12b-14)
	an exhortation to honor God instead of seeming above it (Jer 13:15-17)
	a threat to the king and the queen mother (Jer 13:18-22)
	a question about whether the people can change (Jer 13:23-27)

JEREMIAH 14–17 BEGINS: THINK ABOUT PRAYER

Jeremiah 14–17 opens by describing how Judah is praying in the midst of a crisis brought by drought and reveals that Yahweh is not moved to action by their prayer: indeed, he tells Jeremiah not to pray for them anymore.

Judah mourns,
> its settlements languish.
People look down to the ground,
> Jerusalem's crying goes up. (Jer 14:2)

If our wayward acts avow against us, Yahweh,
> act for the sake of your name.

> Because our turnings away are many;
>> we've done wrong to you.
> Israel's hope,
>> its deliverer in time of pressure,
> Why should you become like an alien in the country,
>> like a traveler who turns aside to lodge?
> Why should you become like someone bewildered,
>> like a strong man who can't deliver?
> But you're among us, Yahweh,
>> your name has been called out over us, don't let go of us. (Jer 14:7-9)

The rains have failed and people can't find water to drink, give to their animals, or irrigate their crops. It's a desperate situation. So it makes people pray. While they know that the rains failing is sometimes "one of those things," not a punishment, on this occasion they pray as people who recognize that natural disasters can be a way God confronts us about our waywardness and tries to pull us back. Their acknowledgment that they have turned away from God is one thing they get right about their prayer.

The other thing is the way they appeal to God. They appeal to him for the sake of his name. Someone's name stands for who they are (see section "Jeremiah 7–10 Begins: Think About the Temple" above). When you say someone's name, it conjures up the person in your mind. Parents are commonly thoughtful about the name they give their child. It's not random. It says something. My names, John Edgar, are my grandfather's and my father's names. In traditional societies, sometimes the name tells you something about the commitments the parents attach to the person: Zedekiah means "Yahweh is my faithfulness" (if only he believed it was true). In Exodus 3, Yahweh told Moses that his name meant he is the God who will always be there for him and for Israel. The name sums up the character: it indicates who you are. In addition, we think of people having a good name or a bad name, a good reputation or a bad reputation. So people appeal to Yahweh to act "for the sake of your name": because of who you are and because of what people will think of you if you don't act.

In a more original version of the argument, on this occasion people remind Yahweh that because of who he is, he is their "hope," which means "their deliverer in a time of pressure" like the present crisis. Even more originally and boldly, on the other hand, they note that he's behaving like a random passerby who has no obligation to the country he's passing through, or like a warrior who's forgotten how to take decisive action. Such arguments might seem disrespectful, but First Testament prayers often work in that way, and people never get rebuked for impertinence. They don't regularly call on God as Father, but they relate to God with the confidence of children who know they can say anything to their father. "You're among us." They go on, "You're like someone strong in the midst of his people." In effect, it's an appeal to the covenant relationship. The same applies to "your name has been called out over us," the phrase that was used of the temple in Jeremiah 7. "You own us." We belong to you. So don't let go of us.

It's a model prayer. How could God resist it? With ease, apparently, because he can see the disparity between their words and their lives, and he has no sense that the words indicate any real change in them.

> Yahweh has said this to this people:
> Yes, they've loved straying,
> > they haven't restrained their feet.
> Given that Yahweh doesn't accept them,
> > he'll now be mindful of their waywardness
> > and he'll attend to their wrongdoings. (Jer 14:10)

God accepts us as we are, right? Not so much: "Yahweh doesn't accept them." Honest prayer works, even if it's brashly impolite. Dishonest prayer doesn't work, even if it's gracious and uses the right words. Did they know they were being dishonest or were they fooling themselves? It's safer to assume that people were fooling themselves because that assumption encourages the readers of the Jeremiah scroll to self-examination.

Yahweh's stance corresponds to the one he threatened to take in his confrontation about the pledge. "They'll cry out to me but I won't listen to them" (Jer 11:11). It's hard to imagine that Yahweh would be able to resist a real turning to him in prayer, but that kind of turning was not what he had in mind. After all, he went on, "Judah's towns and Jerusalem's inhabitants will go and cry out to the gods to whom they've been burning offerings" (Jer 11:12). The test of their genuineness will be, how will they react when I don't answer their prayers? Yahweh knows the answer. They will go back to those other deities. Which will show that their crying out to Yahweh doesn't represent a real turning.

If Yahweh's direct message to people in Jeremiah 14 is frightening, his footnote to Jeremiah is more frightening.

Yahweh said to me, "Don't plead for good things on behalf of this people. When they fast, I won't be listening to their chant. When they make a burnt sacrifice

or offering, I won't be accepting them. Because by sword, by famine, and by
epidemic I'm going to finish them off." (Jer 14:11-12)

Praying for their people is a key aspect of a prophet's vocation, as it is a key
aspect of a minister's vocation. A prophet is someone who takes part in God's
meetings with his cabinet (see sections "Party to Yahweh's Intentions" and
"Identified with Yahweh" in chap. 8 below). That's how a prophet knows what
God has decided to do and how he has commissioned other members of the
cabinet (his envoys or aides) to go and do it. But also, the prophet is in a position to take part in the debates that lead to the making of a decision. That
taking part is what we call prayer. On this occasion, Yahweh points out to
Jeremiah that the cabinet has come to its decision, so he needs to shut up so
they can move to the next business.

It's not the first time that Yahweh has told Jeremiah not to pray for the
people either (see Jer 7:16; 11:14). Why does he keep saying it? Is he not sure
whether he means it? Is he not sure Jeremiah thinks he means it? Does Jeremiah take no notice and keep urging the meeting not to move on to next
business?—meetings sometimes work that way. Does Jeremiah take into account a conviction that Yahweh may have a hard time resisting such prayers?

If you are the people to whom Jeremiah is revealing what God has said to
him, you would be unwise to make that assumption. We need to consider not
only why Yahweh keeps saying it but why the Jeremiah scroll keeps telling
people that Yahweh has said it. Judah needs to know what Yahweh is saying
about his attitude toward prayer; it might be something to drive Judah to its
senses. At the moment, it's ridiculous to think that Judah could simply show
up in the temple for worship, pray, and expect Yahweh to welcome them and
listen. In these circumstances (as Yahweh asked earlier), "What business does
my beloved have in my house?" It will be entirely appropriate for the Babylonians to "make the sacred flesh pass from you" by destroying the temple and
making offerings impossible (Jer 11:15). But not only is God not listening to
your prayer. You're in danger of no longer being prayed for. You'd better
change. Then you can pray and your prophet can pray for you.

The sequence of events repeats itself later in Jeremiah 14.

Have you totally rejected Judah,
    have you renounced Zion with your entire being?
Why have you struck us down
    and we have no one healing us? . . .

Don't disgrace your honored throne;
>be mindful, don't contravene your pledge with us.

Are there any among the nations' hollow beings who make it rain,
>or do the heavens give showers?

You're the one, Yahweh our God, aren't you,
>so we hope in you, because you made all these things. (Jer 14:19, 21-22).

The questions and the exhortations involve some hutzpah and the confessions raise eyebrows. They provoke Yahweh to retort that he wouldn't listen to Moses or Samuel, those famous prayer advocates, if they stood before him in prayer on this people's behalf (Jer 15:1).

Jeremiah 14–17 is a looser collection of messages than some others, but as a whole it unfolds as follows:

14:1–15:21	four more exchanges
	Judah's suffering and its prayer about the drought, and Yahweh's response (Jer 14:1-12)
	Jeremiah's protest about the other prophets, and Yahweh's response (Jer 14:13-18)
	Judah's suffering and its prayer about attacks, and Yahweh's response (Jer 14:19–15:9)
	Jeremiah's protest about his persecutors, and Yahweh's response (Jer 15:10-21)
16:1–17:11	confrontations and warnings
	Yahweh's ban on Jeremiah marrying or grieving (Jer 16:1-13)
	Yahweh's undertakings about a positive future (Jer 16:14-21)
	Yahweh's confrontations based on the kind of sayings that appear in Proverbs (Jer 17:1-11)
17:12-27	another exchange
	Judah's confession about Yahweh's sacred throne and about shaming (Jer 17:12-13)
	Jeremiah's plea about shaming (Jer 17:14-18)
	Yahweh's challenge about the sacredness of the Sabbath and about a throne (Jer 17:19-27)

JEREMIAH 18–20 BEGINS: THINK ABOUT GOD'S SOVEREIGNTY

Throughout the Jeremiah scroll, Yahweh is both declaring that he is bringing calamity on Judah and other peoples and urging people to turn back to him with the implication that such turning could make a difference to their fate. How do the threat and the exhortation relate? Jeremiah 18–20 begins by talking about God's sovereignty and contributes to approaching this question.

> The word that came to Jeremiah from Yahweh: "Set off and go down to a potter's house, and there I'll let you hear my words." So I went down to a potter's house, and there, he was doing work at the stones. If the object were to spoil that he was making with clay, in the potter's hand, he'd make it again into another object, as it was right in the potter's eyes to do.
>
> Yahweh's word came to me: "Like this potter I can do to you, Israel's household (Yahweh's declaration), can't I. There, like clay in the potter's hand, so are you in my hand, Israel's household. Momentarily I may speak concerning a nation or kingdom about uprooting, demolishing and destroying, but that nation concerning which I've spoken may turn back from its bad dealing. I may then relent about the exile that I intended to do to it. But momentarily I may speak concerning a nation or kingdom about building and planting, and it may do what is bad in my eyes so as not to listen to my voice. I may then relent about the good that I said I'd do to it.
>
> "So now, say to Judah's people and Jerusalem's inhabitants, please: 'Yahweh has said this. Here, I'm shaping bad fortune for you. I'm thinking up intentions concerning you. Turn back, please, each person from his bad way, and make your ways and your practices good.' But they'll say, 'It's desperate, because we shall follow our intentions, and we shall act, each person by the bad determination of his mind.'" (Jer 18:1-12)

Jeremiah announces what God intends to make happen. In some ways, to speak of him predicting things may be misleading. God has told him what he intends to do, and Jeremiah passes on the information. Jeremiah's messages are announcements that God is in a position to make through Jeremiah because he is in a position to decide what happens. An invader will march into Judah, besiege Jerusalem, and devastate it. Yahweh is the sovereign Lord, and he can make things happen. What about human "freewill"? The Scriptures don't have a word for freewill and they don't seem agonized by the question of divine sovereignty and human freewill. They simply assume both that God makes decisions about things and that human beings make their decisions and are responsible for their actions.

The story of Jeremiah and the potter suggests some reflection on one aspect of these issues. If Yahweh has made up his mind to bring about the trouble that Judah deserves, what is the point of telling them? If he has made up his mind to restore Judah, does their attitude to his promises make any difference?

Before an execution or a lynching, the person uttering the judgment or doing the killing commonly tells the victim why they are undertaking their action; they do not just do it. Are they reassuring themselves that they are doing the right thing? Is getting a wrongdoer to see the rightness of a punishment one aspect of restoring the balance of the universe that is disturbed by wrongdoing? With Judah, is one of Yahweh's aims to prepare people for living with the aftermath of the disaster? This story indicates that for Yahweh, there is a relationship between declarations of intent and challenges to turn toward faithfulness. It might be an oversimplification to say that the aim of making the declarations is simply to get people to turn. But it is one aim. And whenever Yahweh declares the intention to do something, an "unless" or "if" (spoken, or more often unspoken) accompanies it. Yahweh's promises are implicitly dependent on his people's faithfulness to him. His threats are implicitly dependent on their continuing in their unfaithfulness.

So wherein lies Yahweh's sovereignty? There are several facets to the answer. One is that God isn't very worried about his sovereignty. If you are sovereign, you don't get anxious about it. You know your intentions will come about in the end. Another is that God is more concerned about his relationship with his people than with his sovereignty over them. Another is that God is always happy to take the long view. Time is on his side. Something similar applies to the other aspect of the question of sovereignty and freewill, the one that relates to the people he gets to implement his decisions, the executioners or benefactors as opposed to their victims or beneficiaries. Yahweh intends to "arouse" these agents (Jer 50:9; 51:1, 11), as Yahweh will "arouse" the spirit of the Judahites to get to work on restoring the temple (Hag 1:14). The nearest I have to an idea of how this works is to think about our experience of an idea coming to us about something we might do. When it happens, we don't have to follow up on the idea, but we might follow it up, and we might have a sense that we are being badgered to do so. The idea comes to Nebuchadrezzar to invade Judah and then to Cyrus to attack Babylon (and to the Judahites to rebuild the temple), and they decide to follow it up.

The story of the potter recognizes that they may not do so. The potter works in a flexible fashion. It's as if the clay is alive and has a mind of its own (as Judah and Nebuchadrezzar do). If it doesn't yield to the potter's attempt to make one sort of pot, he abandons that aim and makes it into something else. Yahweh works the same way with Israel. "Momentarily I may speak concerning a nation or kingdom about uprooting, demolishing and destroying"

(Jer 18:7). It's what he did in general terms back at the beginning (Jer 1:10), without any suggestion that he had not determined exactly what was to happen. "But that nation concerning which I've spoken may turn back from its bad dealing. I may then relent about the exile that I intended to do to it" (Jer 18:8). Apparently, no threat is final. It's never over until it's over.

On the other hand, "momentarily I may speak concerning a nation or kingdom about building and planting," as again he did in general terms back at the beginning, "and it may do what is bad in my eyes so as not to listen to my voice. I may then relent about the good that I said I'd do to it" (Jer 18:9-10). The bad news is thus that the converse applies to Yahweh's promises. At least it can apply, though there's no indication that the Judahites in Babylon had turned to Yahweh before he announced that he was now going to bring them back to Jerusalem or before he did make it possible for them to go back. Yahweh's promises about their returning to Jerusalem were not conditional on their turning. But we noted in chapter three that the people would be unwise to rely on the fact that he has difficulty resisting the temptation to be merciful and therefore infer that they need not turn.

If they do turn, they can rely on his commitment to be merciful. "Here, I'm shaping bad fortune for you," like a potter shaping his pot, Yahweh says. "I'm thinking up intentions concerning you. Turn back, please, each person from his bad way, and make your ways and your practices good" (Jer 18:11). The trouble is he knows that they will say, "It's desperate, because we shall follow our intentions, and we shall act, each person by the bad determination of his mind" (Jer 18:12). They don't literally speak in those terms, but they are the implications of their attitude (Jeremiah sometimes puts on people's lips the implications of their attitude). If it is indeed their attitude, why does Yahweh bother? Because for all that he knows, there is another sense in which he always keeps a "perhaps" in the back of his head (Jer 26:3).

Then he will "relent" (*niham*). Jeremiah uses this verb more than anyone, though often in the negative to indicate that Yahweh will not relent (Jer 4:28). Yahweh can get tired of relenting, though he doesn't stop (Jer 15:6). While the translation "repent" (KJV) could be misleading, "change one's mind" is a reasonable rendering as long as we do not infer that Yahweh is fickle. "Change of heart" is closer to the Hebrew word, which especially refers to feelings— other forms of the verb suggest being sorry without implying regret at taking the action in question (Jer 42:10) or suggest finding comfort or giving comfort (Jer 16:7; 31:13).

That first story about a potter and a pot is not the only such story in Jeremiah 18–20, which as a whole unfolds as follows:

18:1-23	the way responses can make a difference to Yahweh's action
	a story about Yahweh's planning and his flexibility, with a gloomy conclusion (Jer 18:1-12)
	Yahweh's assessment of Judah and its inflexibility (Jer 18:13-17)
	their planning against Jeremiah and his consequent protest and prayer (Jer 18:18-23)
19:1–20:18	the way responses may mean it becomes too late
	a story in which Yahweh commissions the smashing of a pot (Jer 19:1-13)
	a continuation of the story confirming Judah's inflexibility (Jer 19:14–20:6)
	Jeremiah's protest and praise, and his cry of despair over Judah (Jer 20:7-18)

JEREMIAH 21–25 BEGINS: THINK ABOUT GOVERNMENT

The Jeremiah scroll has made virtually no mention of the individual kings of Judah since introducing them in Jeremiah 1:1-3. Much of Jeremiah 21–25 now talks about kings. Modern readers need to think of them and their staff as equivalent to our presidents, prime ministers, parliaments, congresses, and senates.

Jeremiah 21:1-10 is a story about Zedekiah, set on the eve of the fall of Jerusalem in 587, in which Jeremiah sets before Zedekiah "the way to life" (surrendering to the Babylonians) and "the way to death" (resisting them). Following that story, the scroll reverts to its practice of not naming kings, which hints that the message applies to any king, though the collocation with the story about Zedekiah suggests that failure to attend to Jeremiah's message about kingship is a factor lying behind the 587 catastrophe.

Yahweh said this: "Go down to the house of the king of Judah and speak there this word. Say, 'Listen to Yahweh's word, king of Judah, you who sit on David's throne and your servants and your people who come through these gateways. Yahweh has said this: "Exercise authority with faithfulness, rescue the person who's been robbed from the hand of the oppressor, don't wrong alien, orphan and widow, don't be violent, don't shed the blood of someone free of guilt in this place. Because if you really do act on this word, then through this house's gateways will come David's kings sitting on his throne, riding chariot and horses, he and his servants and his people. But if you don't listen to these words,

I swear by myself (Yahweh's declaration) that this house will become a waste.""" (Jer 22:1-5)

Whereas Western nations may assume that a government's first obligation is to look after the nation's economic well-being and its defense, ancient Near Eastern peoples put as much emphasis on a king's obligation to safeguard the nation's moral and social order. When a ruler such as Hammurabi came to the throne, he published his law code as a statement of the kind of moral and social principles he was committed to (whether he actually sought to undergird them is of course a different matter, as with election commitments by Western politicians). It fits that assumption that the book of Judges pictures the moral and social disorder of the period it describes as indicating that everyone was doing what was right in their own eyes in a situation when there was no king in Israel. First Samuel 8 has the people urging the appointment of a king because the sons of their leader, Samuel, took bribes in connection with their exercise of authority. In contrast, one of the best things that the narrative ever says about David is that when he has settled down as king, "he exercised authority with faithfulness for all his people" (2 Sam 8:15).

In keeping with this plaudit, Yahweh urges the king in Jeremiah's day to "exercise authority with faithfulness," or more literally, "authority and faithfulness." Traditionally, translations have expressions such as "justice and righteousness," which cover aspects of the phrase, but there is more to it. The first word (*mishpat*) suggests being in a position where you have the power to make decisions and exercise control—to be the government, in fact. The word presupposes that you will do it in a just way, though in itself the word is about power. The second word (*sedaqah*) makes the ethical point explicit. It denotes the kind of righteousness that does the right thing by other people to whom one has obligations. The combination of words suggests an obligation resting on the community as a whole (Jer 4:2)—the head of a household, for instance, must see that decisions are taken in a faithful way within the household and in its relationship with vulnerable people outside, and the community has that obligation because it reflects Yahweh's own nature and way of operating (Jer 9:24). The obligation rests on kings because they have great power and the temptation to misuse it. Jeremiah spells out the point in terms that fit the teaching of the Torah and correspond to that statement about David. The kings' responsibility is to protect rather than take advantage of the powerless, the alien, the orphan, the widow, and the falsely accused;

all could be vulnerable by being robbed of their land or by not having land and therefore having nowhere to live and no way to make a livelihood. Accepting that priority is the surest way to guarantee the stability of the government, because Yahweh will see to it. If the kings behave in accordance with that comment about David, they will continue to reign on their ancestor's throne. But (the implication is) Yahweh's promise to David offers no protection to kings who don't.

Jeremiah continues not to name names, but it isn't difficult to see who he is talking about and talking to.

> Hey, one who builds his house without faithfulness,
>   his lofts without the [proper] exercise of authority!
> He makes his neighbor serve for nothing;
>   he doesn't give him his earnings,
> The one who says, "I'll build myself a vast house,
>   spacious lofts."
> He cuts windows for it, panelled with cedar,
>   painted with vermilion.
> Are you a king
>   because you're competing in cedar?
> Your father—he ate and drank, didn't he,
>   and exercised authority with faithfulness.
> Then things were good for him,
>   when he gave judgement for the weak and needy.
> Then things were good;
>   this is to acknowledge me, isn't it (Yahweh's declaration).
> Because you have no eye or mind
>   except for loot,
> For shedding the blood of the one free of guilt,
>   and for fraud and for extortion. (Jer 22:13-17)

The two contrasting kings, father and son, are Josiah the reformer and his son and successor Jehoiakim the un-reformer. Josiah was committed to the faithful exercise of authority (that phrase recurs from Jer 22:3) and he lived okay but not extravagantly. Jehoiakim lived more in the way people in leadership positions are tempted to live, using his position to enrich the royal coffers and accumulate the resources to build an impressive palace that was appropriate to his position. In doing so, he ignored the deserves of the people who did the work and needed to be paid their wages. Indeed, he was prepared to accumulate resources in shady ways in order to make his own life more in keeping with his position.

Jeremiah 21–25 begins with critique and threat regarding the kings, but it also offers promise (see "David and Levi" in chap. 9 below) and then goes on to cover prophets (see "Jeremiah 26 – 29 Begins: Think about the Reassuring Prophets" in chap. 4 below; see also chap. 8) before coming to chapters that close off the first half of the scroll. Jeremiah 21–25 as a whole thus unfolds as follows:

21:1–23:8	about kings
	a story about Zedekiah (Jer 21:1-10)
	messages for David's household (Jer 21:11–22:9)
	messages about Shallum (Jehoahaz), Jehoiakim, and Coniah (Jehoiachin) (Jer 22:10-30)
	promises about shepherds, a faithful shoot for David, and a new exodus (Jer 23:1-8)
23:9-40	about prophets
24:1-10	about the people exiled in 597 and the people who escaped exile: two baskets of figs
25:1-38	a conclusion to the first half of the scroll and its messages about disaster an implicitly-final warning for Judah and eventual threat to Babylon (Jer 25:1-14) a picture of the warning and threat as a drink from a toxic chalice (Jer 25:15-29) four messages expressing the threat, focusing on the other nations (Jer 25:30-38)

CHAPTER FOUR

THE THEMES IN
JEREMIAH 26-52

✛

IN CHAPTER THREE we looked at the themes in the first half of the
Jeremiah scroll. We come now to the themes in the second half, the half
that's mostly stories about Yahweh's dealings with Judah and with Jeremiah.
Again, we'll start from the way in which aspects of First Testament faith form
the jumping-off point for different sections of the scroll, sometimes making
the discussion of a theme a basis for looking at the way that theme appears
elsewhere in the scroll.

JEREMIAH 26–29 BEGINS: THINK ABOUT
THE REASSURING PROPHETS

While Jeremiah 23:9-40 almost brought the first half of the Jeremiah scroll to
an end with a collection of messages about the prophets, the second half of
the scroll begins with a series of stories about the prophets, set in a message
Yahweh sends through Jeremiah.

> "If you don't listen to me by walking according to the instruction that I've put
> before you, listening to the words of my servants the prophets whom I've been
> sending to you, sending assiduously (but you haven't listened), I shall make this
> house like Shiloh, and make this city a formula of slighting to all the nations of
> the earth." . . .

The priests, the prophets, and the entire people listened to Jeremiah speaking these words in Yahweh's house, and when Jeremiah finished speaking all that Yahweh had ordered him to speak to the entire people, the priests, the prophets and the entire people seized him, saying: "You are definitely to die! Why have you been prophesying in Yahweh's name, 'This house will become like Shiloh, and this city will be waste, without inhabitant'?". . .

Jeremiah said to all the officials and the entire people, "It was Yahweh who sent me to prophesy to this house and to this city all the words that you heard. . . ."

The officials and the entire people said to the priests and to the prophets, "There's no sentence of death, because it was in the name of Yahweh our God that he spoke to us." Some people from the country's elders got up and said to all the congregation of the people, "Micah the Morashtite was prophesying in the days of Hezekiah king of Judah. He said to Judah's entire people:

Yahweh of Armies has said this:
Zion will be plowed as open countryside.
Jerusalem will become heaps of rubble,
the mountain of the house, shrines in the forest.

Did Hezekiah king of Judah and all Judah put him to death at all? Was he not in awe of Yahweh and did he not seek Yahweh's goodwill, so that Yahweh relented of the bad thing that he spoke against them?" (Jer 26:4-9, 12-19)

It's possible to make a distinction between "false prophets" and "true prophets." Jeremiah's way of making that distinction is to speak of "the prophets" and "my servants the prophets." The distinction is roughly one between prophets who speak words of encouragement and prophets who tell the truth. In Jeremiah "the prophets" are usually subject to critique. The key basis for the critique is the fact that they exercise this ministry of encouragement when the people of God need discouragement. They are prophets of shalom, an all-embracing Hebrew word suggesting peace as opposed to war, and well-being as opposed to deprivation (see further "Well-Being" in chap. 6 below). It's possible to be a prophet who promises shalom and be one of Yahweh's servants the prophets, but it's a rare thing. For the moment, all of Yahweh's talk is about disaster. The reference to Shiloh shows that this chapter pairs with Jeremiah 7, which is someone's sermon notes from that occasion for which this chapter gives you the story.

Fortunately for Jeremiah, some people can remember hearing about an incident in Jerusalem that confirms Jeremiah's statement about "Yahweh's servants the prophets." It happened a century before, so no one present was there at the time, but these people's grandparents had told them about it or they had read about it in a scroll of Micah's teaching. Maybe it's significant that they were "some people from the country's elders," if they were not Jerusalemites. Micah was not a Jerusalemite; he had said that Jerusalem was going to be so devastated that it would look like a field for plowing (see Mic 3:12). They didn't execute him, these people point out to the potential lynching assembly. So Jeremiah escaped. But not everyone gets away with being a prophet, the scroll goes on.

> There was also a man prophesying in Yahweh's name, Uriah ben Shemaiah from Kiriath-jearim. He prophesied against this city and against this people in accordance with all Jeremiah's words. King Jehoiakim, all his strong men, and all the officials heard his words, and the king sent to put him to death. (Jer 26:20-21)

Uriah preached the same message as Jeremiah. He got wind of the imminent arrival of the king's henchmen and left via the backdoor while they were knocking at the front door, and caught the first camel train to Egypt, which upon reflection might have been a bad idea. It was the Egyptians who had put Jehoiakim on the throne, and he didn't have difficulty getting Uriah extradited. Being a prophet means risking your life.

It's not just true of disaster prophets. A few decades after Jeremiah, Yahweh really is intending to restore Judah in accordance with promises he gives through Jeremiah. In Isaiah 40–55, there are prophecies that come from those decades, and the prophet who delivered these promises of shalom finds himself in danger of losing his life (Is 50:4-11; 53:1-12). You're the city that habitually kills prophets, Jesus says to Jerusalem (Lk 13:34).

Meanwhile, the Jeremiah scroll itself will shortly be recording promises of shalom from Jeremiah (see Jer 33:6, 9). When might the moment for shalom prophecy come? In 597 the Babylonians attacked Jerusalem, plundered the temple, and took King Jehoiachin and many other people into forced migration to Babylon. So Yahweh had made wrath fall on the city. Maybe the moment might come now? Maybe now there could be restoration and blessing? A contemporary of Jeremiah, a prophet called Hananiah, told people that within two years Yahweh would bring king, people, and temple artifacts back to Jerusalem (see Jer 28). Jeremiah commented that prophets had always spoken of war, disaster, and epidemic. When a prophet speaks of shalom—well (in effect, he says), we'll see. Jeremiah speaks with some hyperbole, as he usually does, though a look through the other prophetic scrolls in the First Testament confirms the broad truth of his words.

Why do prophets speak of trouble rather than shalom, and why can the present circumstances not be an exception? Jeremiah 23:9-40 has already given the answer. Anybody who knows anything about living rightly or about God can look at the people of God and see that they have gone wildly astray. How could God possibly be promising shalom to them? Therefore, anyone who has taken part in meetings of Yahweh's cabinet, as Jeremiah has, couldn't be bringing the message Hananiah is bringing. Jeremiah is not just appealing to his inner spiritual experience. Hananiah may have believed he had the same inner spiritual experience. Hananiah was sincere in his desire to serve God and fulfill his ministry to his people. But if he did make that claim, he's shown to be deceiving himself, because what he says doesn't correspond to who God is.

Jeremiah 26–29 as a whole with its focus on prophets unfolds as follows:

26:1–27:1a	how Jeremiah the prophet escapes lynching
27:1b-22	how Jeremiah urges Judah not to listen to the prophets
28:1-17	how Hananiah the prophet confronts Jeremiah the prophet and loses his life
29:1-32	how Jeremiah urges the exiles not to believe their prophets and to settle down

JEREMIAH 30–33 BEGINS: THINK ABOUT RESTORATION AND RETURNING

Jeremiah 30–33 brings a change in the scroll as for a while it talks about the future in an encouraging way. Whereas Jeremiah previously confronted the likes of Hananiah, in relation to the other side of catastrophe he can talk in a similar way to Hananiah: "Days are coming (Yahweh's declaration) when I shall restore the fortunes of my people Israel and Judah, Yahweh has said" (Jer 30:3). "Restore the fortunes" or "bring about the restoration" (*shub shebut*) is a favorite Jeremiah expression. Etymologically it means "turn [back] the turning [back], which could make one think of returning from exile, and enabling people to return from exile is an important aspect of restoring Israel. Indeed, Yahweh goes on, "and I will enable them to return to the country that I gave their ancestors, and they will possess it" (Jer 30:3; cf. Jer 29:14).

Later, Jeremiah reports:

> A voice makes itself heard in Ramah,
>> lamentation, bitter crying.
> Rachel is crying over her children;
>> she's refused to find comfort over her children,
>> because they're not there. (Jer 31:15)

Rachel died in giving birth to Benjamin and she was buried somewhere on the family's journey back to Canaan from Jacob's self-imposed exile (Gen 35:16-20). Jeremiah pictures her, in the tomb that people would know about, grieving over the fact that her "children" are now trudging off past her into their exile. But Yahweh responds to her:

> Restrain your voice from crying
>> and your eyes from tears.
> Because there will be a reward for your work (Yahweh's declaration);
>> they will return from the enemy's country.
> There is hope for your future (Yahweh's declaration);
>> your children will return to their territory. (Jer 31:16-17)

Twice that verb *return* recurs. People will need more than a geographical return to their ruined city and country. They will need their homes and city rebuilt.

> Here am I, I'm going to restore the fortunes of Jacob's tents,
>> and on his dwellings I shall have compassion.
> A city will be built on its tell;
>> a citadel will sit on its authorized place. (Jer 30:18)

As someone from Anathoth with his family's land there, Jeremiah knows that the country as a whole needs more than the rebuilding of Jerusalem.

> They will again say this thing
>> in the country of Judah and in its towns,
>> when I restore their fortunes:
> "May Yahweh bless you,
>> faithful abode, sacred mountain."
> Judah and all its towns together will dwell in it as farmers,
>> and people will go about with the flock.
> Because I'm saturating the weary person
>> and filling everyone who languishes. (Jer 31:23-25)

The relationship of city and country can be tricky—city can oppress country and country can resent city. But part of Yahweh's restoration will be the renewing of Zion itself as Yahweh's abode, and the country people will rejoice in it. Yahweh will renew their land that was devastated by army invasion, occupation, and despoiling, and will reestablish the viability of their lives as farmers, shepherds, and landholders (cf. Jer 32:44). He will restore the joy of family life, community life, and worship life:

> A voice will make itself heard in this place of which you're saying, "It's desolate, without human being, without animal, in Judah's towns and in Jerusalem's devastated courtyards, without human being, without animal," the voice of joy and of celebration, the voice of groom and of bride, the voice of people saying, "Confess Yahweh of Armies, because Yahweh is good, because his commitment lasts permanently," bringing a thank-offering to Yahweh's house, because I shall restore the country's fortunes as before. (Jer 33:10-11)

The restoring of fortunes will include the reestablishing of Davidic leadership (Jer 33:26). And the restoring of fortunes will apply to countries such as Moab, Ammon, and Elam too (Jer 48:47; 49:6, 39). Perhaps it will be an aspect of the effect on other peoples as Israel is restored:

> I'm going to make recovery and healing grow up for it. I shall heal and reveal to them abundance of well-being and truth. I shall restore Judah's fortunes and Israel's fortunes and build them up as before. I shall purify them from all their waywardness with which they did wrong to me, and I shall pardon all their wayward acts with which they did wrong to me and rebelled against me. For me it will mean a name to celebrate, and praise and splendor, for all the nations of the earth that hear of all the good things that I'm going to do with them, and they will be in awe and will shiver because of all the good things and all the well-being that I'm going to do for it. (Jer 33:6-9)

The restoring will be external, material, and physical. It will also be internal, moral, and relational. That promise about the nature of the restoring, the returning, links with another way in which Jeremiah speaks of turning and returning. He has talked about Israel turning away and needing to return, and the impossibility of getting people to do so. Here Yahweh pictures the people themselves recognizing the problem. He follows up his report of Rachel lamenting with a report of Ephraim lamenting:

> You've disciplined me and I've undergone discipline
> > like a calf that hadn't been trained.
> Turn me back and I'll turn back,
> > because you are Yahweh my God.

Because after I turned I relented;
> after I came to acknowledge it I struck my thigh.

I was shamed, yes disgraced,
> because I bore the insult of my youth. (Jer 31:18-19)

More than once Jeremiah has imagined Israel saying that its situation is desperate, hopeless; his issuing them with exhortations to change is futile (Jer 2:25; 18:12). Here too they speak with some contradiction—they know they need to turn but they need Yahweh to get them to turn. How could Yahweh resist such a plea?

Ephraim is a dear son to me,
> or a child in whom I took pleasure, isn't he.

Because every time I speak against him,
> I'm so mindful of him again.

That's why my insides moan for him,
> I have deep compassion for him. (Jer 31:20)

Yes, the restoration and the returning of which Jeremiah speaks needs to be both external, material, and physical, and internal, moral, and relational, and Yahweh's compassion will ensure both.

Jeremiah 30–33 as a whole unfolds as follows:

30:1-4	introduction: restoration for Ephraim and Judah
30:5–31:1	Yahweh promises restoration for Judah
31:2-22	Yahweh promises rebuilding for Ephraim
31:23-40	Yahweh promises reversal for Israel as a whole
32:1-44	Jeremiah acquires some land on behalf of his family
33:1-23	Yahweh promises healing, rejoicing, pasturing, compassion, and Davidic/Levite leaders

JEREMIAH 34–36 BEGINS: THINK ABOUT WHAT IS WRITTEN

The Jeremiah scroll has moved from gloom to hope only momentarily. Perhaps the chapters of promise function to make it possible for us to face things getting much worse.

In the title of this section, I cheat slightly, because Jeremiah 34 doesn't explicitly speak of something written down, though it implies it in referring to the rule about freeing bondservants. Exodus 21 is the oldest version of that rule known to us. Deuteronomy 15 is a revised version. The different versions of the rules Yahweh gave Israel, in Exodus and Deuteronomy (and in Leviticus), reflect the need to rework rules in different social contexts. For instance, Deuteronomy takes more account of Israel's development into a more urbanized society in its day. Yahweh makes allowance for that development in inspiring Israel's priests and/or scribes to rework the rules. The Deuteronomy version of the rules makes explicit that they apply to women as well as men, and they appeal to other Israelites being your "brothers" (and sisters); you ought to treat them as part of your extended family. This story includes those notes.

> King Zedekiah solemnized a pledge with the entire people that was in Jerusalem to call to them for a release, for each one to send off his servant and each one his maidservant, the Hebrew man and the Hebrew woman, as free persons, so that they wouldn't serve them, an individual Judahite his brother. All the officials and the entire people that came into the pledge obeyed, by each one sending off his servant and each one his maidservant as free persons, so that they wouldn't serve them anymore.
>
> So they obeyed and sent them off, but afterwards they turned back and got back the servants and the maidservants whom they had sent off as free persons, and subjugated them as servants and maidservants.
>
> Yahweh's word came to Jeremiah from Yahweh: "Yahweh, Israel's God, has said this: 'I myself solemnized a pledge with your ancestors on the day I got them out of the country of Egypt, out of a household of servants, saying, "At the end of seven years you're to send off, each one, his Hebrew brother who has sold himself to you and served you for six years; you're to send him off as a free man from being with you."'" (Jer 34:8-14)

The rules about the release of bondservants were an aspect of the way the social safety net in Israel and among other Middle Eastern peoples was supposed to work. Someone whose family got into economic trouble could indenture their family and themselves to another family to work as bondservants. Modern translations often use the word slave, which is misleading. The theory was that people would work in this other family for a limited period and be supported by it while they got their own life together. The arrangement was taken up in the seventeenth century when thousands of people from Europe who came to the American colonies paid retrospectively for their passage by working for a set number of years for their sponsor.

Such was the theory, though the practice was liable to abuse, and Jeremiah 34 presupposes that householders had not been releasing their bondservants after their years of service with the wherewithal to restart their independent lives. The siege of Jerusalem caused them to release them, perhaps as an act of repentance or because the servants were now more of a liability than an asset. When the siege was temporarily lifted, they took them back (perhaps the servants would be willing to come back precisely because they still had no way of managing on their own).

> "Your ancestors didn't listen to me; they didn't bend their ear. Just now you yourselves turned back and did what was right in my eyes by calling for a release, each one to his neighbor, and you solemnized a pledge before me in the house over which my name has been called out. But you've turned back and profaned my name; you've got back each one his servant and each one his maidservant whom you sent off as free persons to live their life, and you've subjugated them as servants and as maidservants to you."
>
> Therefore Yahweh has said this. "You haven't listened to me by calling for a release, each one to his brother, each to his neighbor. Here am I, I'm going to call for a release to you (Yahweh's declaration)—to sword, to epidemic, and to famine. I'm going to make you a horror to all earth's kingdoms. I'm going to make the people who are transgressing my pledge, who haven't acted on the words in the pledge that they solemnized before me, into the calf that they cut into two and passed between its parts: Judah's officials and Jerusalem's officials, the courtiers, the priests, and the entire people of the country who passed between the parts of the calf." (Jer 34:14-19)

The Jerusalemites have broken their word. It was a promise they made before Yahweh, so in failing to keep it, they have profaned Yahweh's name. They've treated that name as if it was something ordinary. And their promise was solemnized by a powerful rite described in Genesis 15. It involved cutting an animal in two, walking between the parts, and praying that what happened to the animal would happen to them if they didn't keep their word. In effect their reneging on their word leads Yahweh to guarantee that it will happen to them.

Putting things in writing is a serious business. If the rules for Israel's life are in writing, they need to be taken seriously. If Yahweh's message through a prophet is put into writing, it has to be taken seriously. The story that soon follows in Jeremiah 36, about the scroll torn up and burned by Jehoiakim, illustrates the point (see "The Word of God at the Critical Moment" in chap. 2 above; Jeremiah sometimes uses the word for "document," *sepher*, and sometimes the word for "scroll," *megillah*, which implies a document that is big enough to need rolling up).

There are several reasons for putting messages into writing. The first is a practical one. Someone else can read out a document on Jeremiah's behalf. He can send Baruch off to read it to the people as a whole, and the document can then be taken to the king. And when Jeremiah has (say) gone off to Egypt or died, his words can still come home to people. Paradoxically, the introduction to the Jeremiah scroll (Jer 1:1-3) refers to what will follow simply as the words of Jeremiah (of which of course it has many, though also many stories about him) and doesn't call itself a document (as the Nahum scroll does). But when Yahweh declares the intention to bring upon Babylon all the words in "this document" (Jer 25:13) he likely refers to the Jeremiah scroll as a whole as it exists at that point. And the aim of Jeremiah's curators in assembling his words in a document is that people read it in the future—as we are doing.

A second reason is implied by the account of the scroll's fate in Jeremiah 36, when the king tears it up and burns it. Spoken words are one thing. They can get lost. They can be denied. Words in writing are another. Putting something into writing makes it more definite. If they are words about the future and statements of intent, they become more certain, more fixed. Jehoiakim knows it; he burns the scroll to stop it from coming true. It's a naive gesture, but it's a meaningful one. It fits that Jeremiah then simply redictates the scroll and adds lots more words to it (that closing note makes one shiver, not least for Jehoiakim). The written word will find fulfillment.

The same rationale applies to Yahweh's commissioning Jeremiah to write down his words in Jeremiah 30. The words that follow there are the promises about restoration. Whether they belong in the dark days just before 587 or the dark years that follow, they would not seem plausible. Yahweh's putting them into writing guarantees them.

The same implication emerges again from the story of Jeremiah writing down his messages about trouble for Babylon.

> The word that Jeremiah the prophet ordered to Seraiah ben Neriah son of Mah-seiah when he went with Zedekiah king of Judah to Babylon in the fourth year of his reign; Seraiah was accommodation officer. Jeremiah wrote down all the bad fortune that would come to Babylon on a document, all these words that are written concerning Babylon.
>
> Jeremiah said to Seraiah, "When you come to Babylon, you're to see that you read out all these words. And you're to say, 'Yahweh, you yourself have spoken concerning this place that you'll cut it off, so that there won't be anyone living in it, human being or animal, because it's to be a great desolation permanently.'
>
> "When you've finished reading out this document, you're to tie a stone to it and throw it into the middle of the Euphrates. You're to say, 'In this way Babylon

will sink and not rise up because of the bad fortune that I'm going to bring on it.'" (Jer 51:59-64)

Jeremiah doesn't say anything about an audience for the reading—it's not like the reading in Jeremiah 36. Or rather, he indicates that the reading is designed for Yahweh to hear. The reading will be a kind of prayer. "Do you remember these words, Yahweh? Well, please implement them." And then Seraiah is to throw the document into the river, perhaps to ensure that no one can get hold of it and burn it, perhaps as a parable of the sinking of Babylon itself.

As an enacted parable, it parallels Jeremiah's other enacted parables such as the strange tale of a pair of shorts in Jeremiah 13 and the commission to break a decanter in Jeremiah 19. That second comparison suggests another insight. We never hear that Jeremiah did break the decanter nor that Seraiah did drown the scroll. Presumably he did, but the scene is left to our imagination as readers. The stories are told for people to hear, read, and imagine. They don't need to include how the commission was fulfilled. It is the writing of the story in the Jeremiah scroll that matters.

Jeremiah 34–36 as a whole unfolds as follows:

34:1-22	a story about Zedekiah during the siege: not taking the Torah seriously
35:1-19	a story from Jehoiakim's time: a reminder about the Rechabites
36:1-32	a story about Jehoiakim himself: not taking the prophetic scroll seriously

JEREMIAH 37–45 BEGINS: THINK ABOUT TRAGEDY AND TRAUMA

Whereas Jeremiah 26–36 was arranged more thematically than chronologically, Jeremiah 37–45 forms a more-or-less chronological account of the events just before and just after the fall of Jerusalem. It offers readers the opportunity to think about tragedy and trauma, which the original readers in the period beginning in the 580s needed to do.

> King Zedekiah ben Josiah became king in place of Coniah ben Jehoiakim; Nebuchadrezzar king of Babylon made him king in the country of Judah. He didn't listen, he or his servants or the people of the country, to Yahweh's words which he spoke by means of Jeremiah the prophet. (Jer 37:1-2)

The story told by the Jeremiah scroll is full of tragedy—not merely in the sense of terrible disaster but in the sense of disaster that falls on people who could have avoided it but instead brought it about unwittingly through their weakness or inaction or action in a way that could seem like the destiny they could not avoid. Jeremiah 37–45 begins with a summary account of Zedekiah's reign that points to the first element in the tragedy: the people carry on the same as they have before. Jeremiah also carries on the same, urging them to give up their fantasy about deliverance from the Babylonians.

> The officials were furious at Jeremiah, struck him down and put him in the prison house, the house of Jonathan the secretary, because they had made it into the jail. When Jeremiah had come to the cistern house and to the cells, and Jeremiah had lived there for many days, King Zedekiah sent and got him, and the king asked him in his house in secret, "Is there a word from Yahweh?" Jeremiah said, "There is," and said, "You'll be given into the hand of the king of Babylon." (Jer 37:15-17)

A second element in the tragedy, then, is that Yahweh kept speaking to his people, and they kept resisting what he had to say, and kept treating Jeremiah in a way that expressed their attitude to Yahweh.

> The officials said to the king, "This man should please be put to death, because by this means he's slackening the hands of the men of battle who remain in this city, and the hands of the entire people, by speaking to them in accordance with these words, because this man isn't seeking the well-being of this people, but something bad." King Zedekiah said, "There, he's in your hand, because the king can't prevail against you in a thing." (Jer 38:4-5)

In some ways, Zedekiah is the most tragic figure in the story. He half knows what he needs to do and keeps being on the verge of doing it, but in the end he can't stand up to the people who are supposed to be his subordinates. In a way, you can't blame him. His own grandfather had been assassinated by his staff, maybe because he tried to go in for the kind of reform that eventually followed in Josiah's day. He himself was never supposed to be king. Two of his brothers had reigned before him and his nephew had been his predecessor. Yet he ended up as the Babylonians' twenty-one-year-old puppet king, torn between them and his gung-ho cabinet and his pesky prophet. He let Jeremiah be put under house arrest or worse and released him; he consulted him and asked him to pray but then ignored his messages. Eventually he engaged in an ignominious but unsuccessful flight, was abandoned by his troops, and was hauled off to Nebuchadrezzar's headquarters. Here is the last we hear of him:

> In the ninth year of Zedekiah king of Judah, in the tenth month, Nebuchadrezzar king of Babylon and his entire force came to Jerusalem and besieged it. . . .

> The king of Babylon slaughtered Zedekiah's sons at Riblah before his eyes, and the king of Babylon slaughtered all the important people in Judah. He blinded Zedekiah's eyes and shackled him in copper chains to bring him to Babylon. (Jer 39:1, 6-7)

After the city's fall, "they sent and got Jeremiah from the prison courtyard and gave him over to Gedaliah ben Ahikam son of Shaphan to let him go out to a house" (Jer 39:14). Among the Judahite leadership, Gedaliah had apparently been more resolute in his support of their submission to Babylon, the policy which Jeremiah advocated. When the destruction of Jerusalem made it effectively uninhabitable, the Babylonians put him in charge of the administration of Judah with a base in Mizpah, a few miles north of Jerusalem. Not surprisingly, there were people of the opposing political view, and he was warned that someone was plotting to assassinate him, but he didn't believe it. Soon he paid for his naivety with his life. The tragedy didn't just affect him. Reprisals had to come from Babylon, and people knew it. The community had the opportunity for a new start, but tragedy continued to unfold, and it overcame people who opposed the plot rather than supported it.

> The entire company, big and small, came up and said to Jeremiah the prophet, "May our prayer for grace please fall before you; plead on our behalf with Yahweh your God on behalf of all this remainder, because we remain a few out of many, as your eyes see us. May Yahweh your God tell us the way by which we should go and what we should do." (Jer 42:1-3)

The tragedy continues in the way they reject Jeremiah's message when he brings it, and take flight to Egypt, not believing the reassurance they received from Yahweh through Jeremiah. There in Egypt things get worse according to the subsequent account of their continuing resistance to Yahweh in Egypt with his threat that they will die out there (though they didn't).

It all shows that Jeremiah too is a tragic figure. You don't have to make mistakes to earn that designation. As far we can tell, he had no ambition for anything but a quiet life in Anathoth, but Yahweh propels him into a fraught and conflicted life that eventually takes him to Egypt too. Through his ministry virtually no one takes any notice of him and eventually he just disappears. It would be nice to think that in Sheol someone maybe wakes him up from time to time and tells him that people are reading his scroll and that sometimes they take notice of it.

His actual story ends with a footnote about Baruch, who might seem another tragic figure. He wanted nothing but a quiet life as a scribe but got propelled into something else. "I'm tired of it," he says, even in 604 (Jer 45:3). But Yahweh promises to protect him.

The events that led up to and followed 587 were traumatic for people like Zedekiah and Gedaliah as well as for Jeremiah and Baruch. They were traumatic for the entire Judahite community, in Judah itself, in Babylon, and in Egypt. And one of the functions of the work of Jeremiah and his curators and storytellers after 587 would have been to support people as they lived with their trauma. Paradoxically, they would have the capacity to help them live with their trauma simply by telling the terrible story, but also by enabling people to see that the catastrophe had been deserved (or at least it had meaning) yet had actually turned out less terrible than Yahweh's threats warned, and by laying out Yahweh's promises.

The sequence in Jeremiah 37–45 as a whole unfolds as follows:

37:1-21	Zedekiah asks Jeremiah what is going to happen, but ignores him and puts him in jail
38:1-28	Zedekiah's staff put Jeremiah in a worse jail; Zedekiah consults him again
39:1-14	the city falls and Zedekiah flees in vain
39:15-18	Jeremiah's message for a defender
40:1-12	Jeremiah joins Gedaliah in the new community at Mizpah
40:13–41:18	Ishmael assassinates Gedaliah and the rest of the community flee to Bethlehem
42:1–43:13	they ask for advice but reject it and move to Egypt
44:1-30	Jeremiah's final confrontation, challenge, and warning
45:1-5	Jeremiah's message for his scribe

Jeremiah 46–49 Begins: Think About Egypt

Jeremiah's messages close with a series concerning other nations. Egypt comes first, for several possible reasons. It's where Israel started from and where Jeremiah's messages started in Jeremiah 2. Yahweh brought Israel up to Canaan from there (Jer 2:6), a place of servitude (Jer 34:13), which had been like life in an iron smelter (Jer 11:4). But Jeremiah doesn't here refer to Egypt as an oppressor or enemy; it features as the big neighbor whom Judah was inclined to treat as a potential ally and resource when under pressure from other powers, and thus as the big temptation.

Jeremiah's first reference to Egypt takes us back to the game-changing year 604 (Jer 25:1; 36:1). It relates to "the force of Pharaoh Neco king of Egypt, which was at the River Euphrates at Carchemish, which Nebuchadrezzar King

of Babylon struck down in the fourth year of Jehoiakim ben Josiah King of
Judah" (Jer 46:2).

> It's Egypt that rises like the Nile
>> and like streams whose water surge.
> It said, "I'll rise, I'll cover the earth,
>> I'll obliterate a city and the people who live in it." (Jer 46:8)

It was the second great engagement between Egypt and Babylon. The first was
the one Jehoiakim's father tried to forestall when he attacked the Egyptians
on their way to support Assyria against the Babylonians and lost his life as
well as the battle (2 Kings 23:29). Maybe the Judahites learned something;
they didn't get involved in such battles again. Neco still has ambitions to carve
out an empire that includes the Mediterranean countries, but Jeremiah knows
that Nebuchadrezzar is destined to be the major power in the area. He has a
vision of the outcome of Neco's venture:

> Why have I seen—they're shattered,
>> they're turning back!
> Their strong men are struck down, they've fled, fled,
>> they haven't turned round, terror is all round. (Jer 46:5)

In warning Judah against relying on Egypt, as usual Jeremiah combines theological and political considerations. It's unlikely that political acumen comes first;
more likely his theological convictions generate his opposition to reliance on
Egypt and his political conviction that this reliance will not pay (Jer 2:18, 36-37).
For the first half of his ministry, Egypt would have looked at least as impressive
a world power as anyone else, with Assyria in decline and with it not being clear
who would come next. The battle at Carchemish was a showdown that would
decide the answer. Jeremiah knows that in this connection it is Babylon, not
Egypt, that is destined to be Yahweh's servant, as he would later put it.

It was the Egyptians who accidentally brought about a relief of the 588 siege,
but Jeremiah also knows that they will be no help in the long run (Jer 37:4-8).
Egypt also appears as a place of refuge, which incidentally doesn't work for
Uriah (Jer 26:21-23), and Jeremiah warns that it won't work for the group on the
run from Mizpah (Jer 42:1–44:30). Their taking refuge there may be the background to the declaration about Nebuchadrezzar coming to strike Egypt down:

> Why has your champion been swept away?
>> —he didn't stand, because Yahweh thrust him down. . . .

There they called Pharaoh king of Egypt,
  a din who has let the appointed time pass. (Jer 46:15, 17)

Two surprising footnotes follow.

Yahweh of Armies, Israel's God, has said: Here am I, attending to Amon of Thebes and to Pharaoh, to Egypt, to its gods, to its kings—to Pharaoh and to the people who rely on him. I shall give them into the hand of the people who seek their life, into the hand of Nebuchadrezzar king of Babylon and into the hand of his servants. But afterwards it will dwell as in former days. (Jer 46:25-26)

One is thus that in due course Egypt "will dwell as in former days." The other is that Yahweh will deliver Israel from its captivity.

But you, don't be afraid, my servant Jacob;
  don't shatter, Israel.
Because here am I, I'm going to deliver you from far away,
  and your offspring from the country of their captivity. (Jer 46:27)

Yahweh's action against Egypt:

- indicates that he is the real God with real power in the world
- shows that Yahweh has an eye on and is engaged with world conflicts
- provides evidence that the Egyptian gods have no real power
- shows that Egypt's pretensions are destined to be exposed
- indicates that Judah is stupid to treat Egypt as a potential ally with real power
- is preliminary to his restoring Egypt in due course

Jeremiah 46–49 goes on to talk about other, smaller peoples in Judah's world. Again, they are not essentially Judah's enemies; they have sometimes been Judah's allies. Yahweh's action against them has the same six-fold significance as his acting against Egypt, though it also hints at giving back to Judah land that some of these peoples have taken. The peoples are:

47:1-7	Judah's neighbor to the west: Philistia
48:1–49:22	Judah's neighbors to the east: Moab, Ammon, Edom
49:23-39	peoples further off to the east: Damascus, Kedar/Hazor, Elam

JEREMIAH 50–51 BEGINS: THINK ABOUT THE EMPIRE

The events that came to a climax in 604 established Babylon as new imperial power. Jeremiah 50–51 talks about this imperial power in a way that mostly applies to any such power. The beginning of his collected messages about Babylon could seem astonishing:

> Tell among the nations, make it heard;
> > lift a banner, make it heard.
> Don't hide it, say, "Babylon is captured,
> > Bel is shamed, Merodak has shattered."
> Its idols are shamed,
> > its fetishes have shattered. (Jer 50:2)

Long before it happened, Jeremiah pictures Babylon as fallen, as he had pictured Jerusalem as fallen before it happened, but with less evidence or likelihood to go on. There is no weakness about Babylon in Jeremiah's lifetime. The first significance of its fall, when it comes, will be the exposure of its god's weakness; Bel and Merodak are both designations for Babylon's chief god, as Yahweh and El Shaddai both designate Israel's God.

How will this unlikely event come about?

> A northern nation has gone up against it,
> > it will make its country a desolation.
> There will be no one living in it;
> > both human being and animal—they have flitted, gone. (Jer 50:3)

This explanation again compares with Jeremiah's comments about the fall of Judah. The picture of the devastating nature of Babylon's fall corresponds to Jeremiah's visions of Jerusalem's fall. The agent is the same, a yet-unnamed invader from the north; later Jeremiah will name Media and its underlings (Jer 51:11, 27-28). While not naming the invader might in both contexts indicate uncertainty, it also makes for drama, and it makes a theological point: each northern invader is an embodiment of the same supernatural agency under Yahweh's control. Yet further, as Jerusalem's fall was less devastating than Yahweh threatened, so was Babylon's (in fact, much less so), which also indicates that the portrait is a dramatic, imaginative picture, something larger than life rather than a prediction, and suggests that the portrait belongs to the early or mid-500s rather than being painted in light of the event.

Whereas Yahweh's acts against the other countries mostly did not link with their relationship with Judah, the dynamics of Judah's relationship with Babylon are different. "In those days and at that time," the time of Babylon's fall, Yahweh declares,

The Israelites will come,
> they and the Judahites together.

They'll go, and cry as they go,
> and seek Yahweh their God.

They'll ask the way to Zion,
> and their faces will be towards there. (Jer 50:4-5)

Babylon's fall will make possible the Judahites' return to Zion, and even the return of Ephraimites who are still living in the old Assyrian version of the empire. While Yahweh's action against Babylon is again a demonstration of his power in the world and his sovereignty over an imperial power, and of the feebleness of other gods and their hollow images, it is also a means of effecting that restoration of which Jeremiah 30–33 spoke. People like the Babylonians could have said, we won't have acted wrongly in acting against the Judahites: "they did wrong to Yahweh, the faithful abode, their ancestors' hope, Yahweh" (Jer 50:7). Their argument would have been justified, but Yahweh does not accept the implication that therefore there will be no restoration of Judah. What the exiles now have to pay attention to is:

Flit from within Babylon,
> get out of the country of the Chaldeans,
> be like the he-goats before the flock. (Jer 50:8)

Most Judahites will have no desire to "return" to the country they had never seen (it was their parents or grandparents who were the actual forced migrants). Jeremiah urges them to take the lead in leaving—partly to avoid getting caught in the crossfire.

In another contrast with the drift of the prophecies concerning other peoples, Yahweh will be putting Babylon down because of its action against him.

Line up against Babylon round about,
> all you who direct a bow.

Shoot at it, don't hold back with an arrow,
> because it's done wrong to Yahweh.

Shout against it round about, it's giving its hand,
> its towers are falling,

Its walls are being torn down,
> because that is Yahweh's redress. (Jer 50:14-15)

Jeremiah spells out the nature of that wrongdoing when he speaks of redress for his "palace," which Nebuchadrezzar destroyed (Jer 51:11). Perhaps he also does so when he speaks of the empire's action against Israel:

> Israel is scattered sheep
>> that lions have driven away.
> As first the king of Assyria consumed him,
>> then as last Nebuchadrezzar king of Babylon crushed his bones.

Therefore Yahweh of Armies, Israel's God, has said this:

> "Here am I, I'm going to attend
>> to the king of Babylon and to his country
>> as I attended to the king of Assyria." (Jer 50:17-18)

> You were my club,
>> my battle instruments. . . .

> But I shall make good to Babylon
>> and to all Chaldea's inhabitants
> For all their bad dealing,
>> which they did in Zion before your eyes. (Jer 51:20, 24)

The fact that Babylon acted unwittingly as Yahweh's agent does not mean it gets a pass when Yahweh thinks about its own reasons for its action.

As a whole, the Babylon chapters unfold as follows:

50:1–51:58	messages about Babylon
	the fall of Babylon and its rationales (Jer 50:1-20)
	commissions to Babylon's attackers and more rationales (Jer 50:21-32)
	threats against Babylon reworking earlier prophecies (Jer 50:33-46)
	Yahweh's declarations of intent and a song of praise (Jer 51:1-19)
	Yahweh's declarations of intent, naming his agents (Jer 51:20-33)
	Zion's protest about Nebuchadrezzar and Yahweh's response (Jer 51:34-44)
	exhortations to leave Babylon (Jer 51:45-58)
51:59-64	Jeremiah commissions the sinking of another scroll

PART 2

THE
THEOLOGY
OF THE
JEREMIAH SCROLL

In chapters three and four we have considered themes that emerge as we read the Jeremiah scroll section by section, focusing on the messages or stories that open each section. What emerges from the scroll as a whole when we give just as much attention to the rest of each section? What impression does one get of Yahweh as God, of Israel as the people of God, of the nature of wrongdoing, of what prophets are, and of the way God may make the future work out for good or ill?

CHAPTER FIVE

GOD

Yahweh is Israel's God and Israel is Yahweh's people. Who is this God? Much is summed up in a confession about Yahweh set in the midst of an exhortation to Judahites not to be overwhelmed by the theological convictions of their impressive and more cultured overlords in Babylon:

> Yahweh is the true God,
> > he's the living God, the everlasting King.
> At his fury, earth shakes;
> > nations can't cope with his condemnation. (Jer 10:10)

At greater length it's expressed in this confession:

> Oh, Lord Yahweh! There—you made the heavens and the earth by your great energy and your bent arm. Nothing is too extraordinary for you, one who acts with commitment to thousands but makes good for the waywardness of parents into the lap of their children after them: big strong man God (Yahweh is his name), big in counsel and mighty in deed, you whose eyes are open to all the ways of human beings to give to each person in accordance with his ways. (Jer 32:17-19)

It's spelled out in acknowledging Yahweh as master, director, teacher, husband, and creator.

MASTER, KING

In the Jeremiah scroll, the first thing we learn about God is that he assumes the authority to order people around. He is tough, he is not someone you can resist, and he is not someone to mess with. In commissioning Jeremiah as prophet, he does not speak as if he is offering a position Jeremiah can accept or decline but telling him about a decision he made before Jeremiah was born. He has made Jeremiah sacred (Jer 1:5)—that is, he has claimed Jeremiah as someone who is to belong especially to him, as he claimed the Sabbath as a day that especially belongs to him. He overrides Jeremiah's objections while assuring him that he himself will see that things work out.

What applies to Jeremiah applies to prophets in general—the good guys, that is. Yahweh is their master, they are Yahweh's "servants" (Jer 7:25; 25:4; 26:5; 29:19; 35:15; 44:4). The nature of the relationship links with the prophets' common way of speaking. Like the servants of an earthly master, such as a king, who are the envoys taking the king's message and proclaiming, "the king has said this," prophets are envoys who go with King Yahweh's message and proclaim, "Yahweh has said this." In that connection, Jeremiah has a distinctive way of referring to Yahweh's dedication and persistence in sending prophets. People often make an early start when they are doing something they are committed to (e.g., Gen 19:2, 27; 21:14; 22:3). Jeremiah uses this expression of Yahweh: he "has been sending to you all his servants, sending urgently/assiduously" (*shakam*), as if he were getting up early to do it (e.g., Jer 7:13, 25; 11:7; 25:4).

Yahweh's "servants" also include an Israelite king such as David (Jer 33:21, 26) and the Babylonian king (Jer 25:9; 27:6; 43:10). They serve "the Lord Yahweh" (Jer 32:17): "lord" (*adon*) is a regular term for human kings as for the divine king (e.g., Jer 37:20; 38:9). Bringing offerings to Yahweh's palace is a sign of acknowledging Yahweh as king, though it won't be effective if people are concealing other actions that indicate rebellion against the king (Jer 7:21-23).

> Here is the sound of my dear people's cry for help
> > from the country far away:
> 'Isn't Yahweh in Zion,
> > or isn't its King in it?' (Jer 8:19)

They think that having the king in their midst is their protection, which it's supposed to be; but if they haven't been treating him as king, then . . .

The smart thing is to acknowledge Yahweh (Jer 9:23-24), which implies submitting oneself to him. Ironically, however, a claim to acknowledge Yahweh commonly appears when people are implicitly questioning his lordship or behaving as if it is not a reality (cf. Jer 32:25), like Jeremiah on the occasion of his commission (Jer 1:6; see also Jer 2:19, 22; 4:10; 7:20; 14:13; 44:26; 46:10, 10; 49:5; 50:25, 31).

Jacob-Israel too is Yahweh's servant (Jer 30:10; 46:27, 28). While the Ten Commandments speak of Yahweh getting Israel out of a life lived in a house of serfs and thus releasing them from servitude (Ex 20:2; Deut 5:6), in a sense they don't mean he made them free, and Jeremiah never uses that language. What Yahweh really did was make Israel his servant instead of Pharaoh's. Likewise in connection with Nebuchadrezzar, Yahweh declares:

I shall break his yoke from on your neck
  and tear off your straps.
They won't serve foreigners any more with it,
  but they will serve Yahweh their God,
And David their king,
  whom I shall set up over them. (Jer 30:8-9)

A yoke is not a hard thing to wear (Mt 11:28-30). The wise farmer makes sure it fits well and enables the ox to do its work. Being a servant is thus great if you have a good master. When Jesus dies to make people free, what he really does is make them servants of God.

While servants can become the victims of their masters (Jer 34:8-16), being a servant or houseboy should be a secure and honored position; Yahweh thus asks incredulously why the servant has become plunder (Jer 2:14). You can't mess with the master's servant, as you can't mess with the master. The master-servant relationship is one of solemnity and seriousness but also of privilege and security. It's a two-way bond. The servant is committed to the master; the master is committed to the servant. Servants can make requests of their master, for themselves or for others. A servant has privileged access to the master.

Despite the expressions of his toughness, Yahweh does not behave toward Jeremiah like a general giving orders to his troops. He engages in persuasion. The stories of Yahweh and Jonah, and of Jesus and some people he bade to follow him, suggest that Jeremiah might have been able to walk away from Yahweh's commission; for all we know, there were people who did so. While he is prepared to override Jeremiah's reasons for resistance, now and later

Yahweh engages with them. His relationship with Judah is similar. Giving Jeremiah the vision of the seething pot (Jer 1:13) is designed to avoid having to pour it out. The vast bulk of the task Yahweh gives to Jeremiah is a task of persuasion, to try to get Judah to turn around so that destructive action can be cancelled.

DIRECTOR, AUTHORITY FIGURE

The trouble is, Israel the ox has broken its yoke, torn off its straps, and said, "I won't serve" (Jer 2:20). The charge applies to ordinary people and to important people:

> I myself said,
>> "They're only the poor who act foolishly,
> Because they don't acknowledge the way of Yahweh,
>> the authority of their God.
> I'll go to the big people
>> and speak with them." . . .
> Yet those people had altogether broken the yoke,
>> torn off the straps. (Jer 5:4-5)

Jeremiah here introduces the image of Yahweh's "way" or "path," the path that leads to good things (Jer 6:16). It's the path laid out by Yahweh that he himself walks and that they should follow by "going after" him. They shouldn't follow the nations' path (Jer 10:2) and certainly not their own:

> I acknowledge, Yahweh,
>> that an individual's road doesn't belong to him.
> It doesn't belong to a person walking
>> to set his step. (Jer 10:23)

Jeremiah's point isn't that people don't have the metaphysical freedom to make decisions, that they don't have "freewill" (see "Jeremiah 18–20 Begins: Think About God's Sovereignty" in chap. 3 above). It's that they don't have the relational, moral, or religious freedom. Parents are not free to spend their money on indulgences for themselves rather than on food for their children; husbands and wives are not free to get into sexual relationships with other women or men. Their path doesn't belong to them anymore; they are not free to determine their step. Israel's obligation to Yahweh is analogous. Israel doesn't have that freedom. Yahweh decides its direction.

Recognizing or acknowledging Yahweh's path is key to acknowledging or recognizing him as Lord. The word for "acknowledge" (*yada'*) is generally and often rightly translated "know," but it implies not just grasping something with one's mind but admitting and accepting it in one's life. Acknowledging Yahweh as the one who directs his people's path means not only perceiving the direction he is pointing but walking that way, acknowledging his decision-making authority (*mishpat*).

Yahweh's directing means his issuing his rulings (*mishpatim*) in relation to Israel (Jer 1:16). Jeremiah's tough message then corresponds to his own tough commission. It is "to uproot and to pull down, to obliterate and to tear down" before it is "to build and to plant" (Jer 1:10). The destructive action gets twice as much space as the constructive. The balance in the scroll as a whole is even more negative. The vision of the pot pouring out its scalding contents on Jerusalem and Judah says nothing about building and planting. Jeremiah imagines disaster coming and urges Judah,

> On account of this, wrap on sack,
>   lament and howl:
> "Yahweh's angry blazing
>   isn't turning back from us." (Jer 4:8)

The phrase "angry blazing" recurs (e.g., Jer 4:26; 12:13; 25:37).

Fortunately, similar double resonances apply to the idea of authority as they apply to the idea of being master. It is common to speak of God "judging" Israel and of the fall of Jerusalem as an act of "judgment," but this talk can be misleading. The Hebrew word translated as "judge" (*shophet*), which is related to that word for decision-making authority, is the word for the judges in the book of Judges. They were more like saviors than judges. They were people who acted decisively to rescue their people. When Jeremiah promises a coming David who will exercise "judgment" (*mishpat*; Jer 23:5-8), he's talking about him ruling or governing or exercising authority, but like other prophets, Jeremiah pairs "authority" with "faithfulness" in connection with Yahweh as in connection with human authority (see "Jeremiah 21–25 Begins: Think About Government" in chap. 3 above). It's possible to be unfair or self-centered in exercising authority, but Yahweh doesn't act that way. His exercise of authority is good news, if you aren't a rebel against it.

TEACHER, DISCIPLINARIAN

Like the word for the exercise of decisive authority that gets translated as "judgment," the word *torah* collects unfortunate implications in English, through being translated as "law." *Torah* belongs even less in the law court than *mishpat* does. It means instruction or teaching. Yahweh is Israel's insightful, smart teacher, the one who established the world by his insight (Jer 10:12; 51:15), who knows what he is talking about when he tells people how to live. In that reference to the path on which he seeks to direct people (Jer 5:4-5), "way" stands in parallelism with *torah*. Yahweh can point out the path to life and the path to death (Jer 21:8). After Gedaliah's assassination, the group with Jeremiah acknowledge it when they ask Jeremiah to get Yahweh to show them the way (Jer 42:3), though they don't follow his instructions; they thus act in keeping with the usual pattern. They reject Yahweh's teaching or instruction (Jer 6:19). They abandon his teaching and decline to walk by it (Jer 9:13; 26:4; 32:23; 44:10, 23).

In a traditional society like Israel, the main responsibility for teaching rests on parents, and when Jeremiah talks about parents, he thinks of them as the people who guide and teach their children. So teaching is a role of God as Father. "I myself had said, 'How gladly I'll put you among my children and give you a desirable country, the most splendid domain of the nations. I said you'd call me "Father," and not turn back from following me'" (Jer 3:19). They did turn back. But Yahweh didn't give up on the idea:

> I shall lead them to streams of water
>   by a straight way on which they won't collapse.
> Because I've been a father to Israel,
>   and Ephraim is my firstborn. (Jer 31:9)

Ephraim is the northern kingdom that had split off centuries before and gone after other deities more persistently than Judah, but that rebellion didn't mean Yahweh gave up the idea of treating them as his firstborn.

Perhaps it is because he is like a parent or teacher that he is long-tempered (Jer 15:15). Parents and teachers have to be, though Jeremiah is worried about it; it might mean Yahweh fails to do something about the attacks on Jeremiah by people from his neighborhood. Because the trouble is, people can take advantage of his long-temperedness, his inclination to mercy and forgiveness, as Father:

> Now you've called to me, haven't you,
>   "Father, you're the partner of my youth!" (Jer 3:4)

In light of that relationship, they ask themselves:

> Does he hold on to things permanently
>   or keep watch for all time? (Jer 3:5)

Surely not! But Yahweh is the victim of familial unfaithfulness:

> They, their kings, their officials,
>> their priests, their prophets,
> Were saying to a piece of wood, "You're our father,"
>> to some stone, "You gave me birth."
> Because they turned their back to me,
>> not their face. (Jer 2:26-27)

Being long-tempered is a characteristic of Yahweh going back to his self-definition at Sinai (Ex 34:6), and in general Jeremiah is the poster child for Yahweh's long-temperedness. In 604, Yahweh points out to Judah that he has been pressing them through Jeremiah for twenty-three years, though Jeremiah hasn't been the only one (Jer 25:1-6). And it will be nearly another two decades before he finally says, "That's it."

Teaching and discipline are related. The father figure of a certain Israelite kin group imposed on his family a commitment to maintaining the simple life of Israel's time in the wilderness (no building houses, no drinking wine), and they maintained it. Yahweh asks, "Won't you accept discipline by listening to my words" in the same way? (Jer 35:13).

> Accept discipline, Jerusalem,
>> so that I myself don't withdraw from you,
> So that I don't make you a devastation,
>> a country not inhabited. (Jer 6:8)

> With empty results I struck down your children;
>> they didn't accept discipline. (Jer 2:30; cf. Jer 5:3; 7:28; 17:23; 32:33)

My son's math teacher once told us that he could have made my son into a good mathematician, "but we're not allowed to use the slipper nowadays" (*slipper* is British English for "paddle"!).

HUSBAND, PROVIDER

In the main body of the Jeremiah scroll, the first thing we learn is that the relationship of Yahweh and Israel is like a marriage. Yahweh remembers the commitment (*hesed*) and love (*ahabah*) that originally characterized Israel (Jer 2:2). While these two nouns thus first appear in connection with Israel's attitudes, theologically they belong first to Yahweh; all the other references to commitment in the Jeremiah scroll attribute these qualities to Yahweh. The two words come spectacularly together in Jeremiah 31:3:

With permanent love I loved you;
    therefore I've drawn you out with commitment.

This permanent love contrasts with the love that only temporarily characterized Israel. More literally, it is a "love of age" ('*olam*), a love that goes back
as far as you can go and will continue as long as you continue. And the commitment is one that drew Israel through the wilderness to the promised land
and has been drawing it along since. Jeremiah picks up Yahweh's references
to commitment at Sinai (Ex 20:6; 34:7) as "one who acts with commitment to
thousands" (Jer 32:18), which in the context suggests thousands of generations
as it contrasts with allowing or causing the consequences of wrongdoing to
extend just to the next generation or three in the family through the influence
of parents on children and grandchildren. While Yahweh threatens to ter-
minate his commitment and thus to silence in the community the sound of
joy and celebration, such as the rejoicing of a wedding (Jer 16:5; cf. Jer 7:34;
25:10), he can't maintain this stance: Jerusalem will again resound with "the
voice of joy and celebration, the voice of groom and bride, the voice of people
saying, 'Confess Yahweh of Armies, because Yahweh is good, because his
commitment lasts permanently ["to the age," *leolam*]'" (Jer 33:11).

In Jeremiah there are just those two references to "love" in positive contexts
and with possibly romantic connotations (Jer 2:2; 31:3). References to love
mostly allude to people's love for objects other than Yahweh (e.g., Jer 2:25, 33;
8:2; 22:20, 22; 30:14). In urging people to think about the exodus (see "Jeremiah 2–6 Begins: Think About the Exodus" in chap. 3 above), Yahweh starts
with Israel's unfaithfulness and his disappointment at the contrast between its
original commitment and the let-down that followed. He doesn't profess to
be hurt, but he does imply chagrin, bafflement, and thwarted hopes. He is like
a husband or wife who made a marital commitment and had their expectations disappointed by the other person's unfaithfulness. Like a human being
in that situation, he is not just disappointed but steaming with anger and
determined on redress unless there is some change. A judge's responsibility is
to be cool and objective in order to see that justice is done. Yahweh is more
the victim of marital unfaithfulness than the judge. He has conflicted feelings
about Judah. He would like simply to walk out on them.

If only I could have a travellers' lodge in the wilderness,
    and abandon my people, go from them.
Because all of them are adulterers,
    a pack of people breaking faith. (Jer 9:2)

In a way he has.

> I have abandoned my household,
>   I have deserted my domain.
> I have given my dearly beloved
>   into her enemies' fist.
> My domain has become to me
>   like a lion in the forest.
> She's given her voice against me;
>   therefore I've been hostile to her. (Jer 12:7-8)

It's an odd reversal. Whereas Yahweh is sometimes a lion attacking Judah, here Judah is a lion attacking Yahweh. His response is to surrender the lion to its enemies. But this lion is also his "dearly beloved," and the action means deserting his own "domain." The image of husband thus combines with the associated image of householder.

> Many shepherds have devastated my vineyard,
>   trampled my share.
> They've made my desirable share
>   into a devastated wilderness. (Jer 12:10)

But it is his action that has brought about this state of affairs.

CREATOR, LORD

Turning to other deities is not only faithless and wrong but stupid, because Yahweh is the whole world's creator, both as the one who originally brought the world into being and as the one who makes it work now. Yahweh is:

> One who made the earth by his energy,
>   established the world by his expertise,
>   by his understanding stretched out the heavens—
> At his giving voice there was a roar of water in the heavens,
>   and he made clouds go up from the end of the earth.
> He made lightning for the rain,
>   made wind come out from his storehouses. (Jer 10:12-13)

Building requires energy or strength, understanding and the capacity to make a plan, and the expertise to implement the plan. Creating the world required all three capacities in spades. It involved stretching out the heavens like a tent and making sure that the earth below was well-established and secure. It would have been a stunning operation to witness. The second half of Jeremiah's words could as easily describe Yahweh's ongoing involvement with creation as storms roar, clouds hurtle across the sky, lightning flashes, and winds hurl. It all comes from him; certainly our experience of those ongoing realities helps us imagine the original version. He made it all happen and he makes it all happen. Therefore,

> It's me that you should be in awe of, isn't it (Yahweh's declaration),
>   and before me that you should tremble,
> The one who set the sand as a boundary for the sea,
>   a permanent limit that it shouldn't pass over.
> Its waves toss but don't overcome,
>   they roar but don't pass over.
> But this people has a defiant and rebellious mind;
>   they've defied and gone.
> They haven't said to themselves,
>   "We must be in awe of Yahweh our God,
> Who gives the rain, the early and later rain at its time,
>   who keeps for us the weeks set for harvest." (Jer 5:22-24)

A fair rhetorical question therefore is:

> Are there any among the nations' hollow beings who make it rain,
>   or do the heavens give showers?
> You're the one, Yahweh our God, aren't you,
>   so we hope in you, because you made all these things. (Jer 14:22)

Judah is asking the question as it is pleading for Yahweh's mercy. It gets a curt reply, despite the truth in what it manipulatively declares, not because of its untruth.

Yahweh's past creative work is a basis for claims in the present. Jeremiah is to give some orders to envoys from neighboring powers, which they are to transmit to their masters: "I'm the one who made the earth, the human beings, and the animals that are on the face of the earth, by my great energy and by my bent arm, and I give it to whoever is right in my eyes." As creator he is in a position to declare: "So now, I'm giving all these countries into the hand of Nebuchadrezzar king of Babylon my servant. Even the creatures of the wild I'm giving him to serve him" (Jer 27:5-6). It's not obvious what it means to give over these creatures to Nebuchadrezzar, but Yahweh's ability to do so issues from his sovereignty as a creator. They had better believe it.

A classic, vivid, concrete way to speak of God's sovereignty in his created universe is to call him "Yahweh of Armies," as Jeremiah does seventy-nine times. The traditional translation is "Lord of hosts," but the expression combines the actual name of God with the ordinary word for armies that appears on the back of an Israeli military truck. He is the God who has under his command all the dynamic, energetic, fierce forces in the universe; no violent, aggressive forces can successfully oppose him. As Yahweh of Armies, he is "big in counsel and mighty in deed" (Jer 32:19). It's therefore stupid that people "didn't listen, they didn't bend their ear, they walked by their own counsels, by the bad determination of their mind" (Jer 7:24). Yahweh is capable of resolving, "I shall pitch out the counsel of Judah and Jerusalem in this place. I shall make them fall by the sword before their enemies" (Jer 19:7), and then of doing it. The same applies (for instance) to the Edomites with their supposed smartness, counsel, and discernment (Jer 49:7), expressed in Jeremiah's day in their designs on Judahite land.

THE CREATOR'S WORLD

There is no mixing up of creation and creator, or of the created world and Israel, or of humanity and nature, but neither is there any separating of them. The universe doesn't have life in itself in the sense of being self-existent, any more than humanity does: "do the heavens give showers?" (Jer 14:22). But it does have life, and it is capable of many of the same activities as humanity. The link between Yahweh and his creation gives it a capacity for perceiving what is right that enables it to respond with horror at Israel's turning to other deities:

> My people have changed my splendour
>   for what doesn't prevail in anything.
> Be devastated at this, heavens,
>   shudder, be utterly desolate. (Jer 2:11-12)

Unfortunately for creation, its association with humanity means it joins in paying the penalty for humanity's turning away.

> For the mountains I shall take up crying and wailing,
>   and for the wilderness pastures a lament.
> Because they're laid waste, with no one passing through,
>   and people don't hear the sound of livestock.
> Both the birds of the heavens and the animals,
>   they've fled; they've gone. (Jer 9:10)

Because of Judah's serving other deities in Jerusalem, "my anger, my fury, is going to pour out on this place, on human beings, on animals, on the trees in the open country and on the fruit of the earth. It will burn up and not go out" (Jer 7:20). Being laid waste by an invading army as a result of Judah's turning away gives creation reason to be mourning for itself as well as being horrified:

> How long will the country mourn,
>> the grass in all the fields wither?
> Through the bad action of the people who live in it,
>> animals and birds come to an end. (Jer 12:4)

Such pictures are nothing compared with the prospect of devastation that amounts to the undoing of creation:

> I looked at the earth and there—it was empty, void;
>> and at the heavens—there was no light in them.
> I looked at the mountains and there—they were quaking,
>> and all the hills were moving to and fro.
> I looked and there—no human being,
>> and every bird in the heavens had fled.
> I looked and there—the farmland was wilderness,
>> and all its towns were burned,
> In the face of Yahweh,
>> in the face of his angry blazing.

> Because Yahweh has said this:

> "The entire country will become desolation
>> (but I won't make an end).
> On account of this the earth mourns,
>> the heavens are dark above." (Jer 4:23-28)

Fortunately there is a whole other link between creation in its relationship to Yahweh and the destiny of Israel. Yahweh is the one who set the laws that govern sun, moon, stars, and tides, and as that God he says,

> If these laws move away from before me (Yahweh's declaration),
>> Israel's offspring may also cease
>> from being a nation for all time. (Jer 31:36)

The natural laws are the consistent ways in which the cosmos operates. The sun rises each day, the moon comes out in the evening, the stars take their regular place in the night sky, because of their relationship to Yahweh—they do it "before me." Israel may take their consistency as a promise of its own consistency. Further,

> If the heavens above may be measured.
> > and earth's foundations below be explored,
> Also I may reject the entire offspring of Israel
> > for what they've done. (Jer 31:37)

People who know more about the dimensions of the cosmos or the depths of the earth may find that promise the more reassuring. While Yahweh can talk about rejecting (Jer 6:30; 7:29), he can also thus here deny its possibility (cf. Jer 33:23-26). The promise applies to Israel as a people; it also works specifically for entities whose future might seem even more uncertain, in respect of Yahweh's pledges to David and his line as kings and to Levi and his line as priests (Jer 33:20-22). Two and a half millennia later those promises are even more eyebrow raising. There is no David reigning and there are no Levites ministering (see "Living In Between" in chap. 9). Yet Yahweh made his creation the guarantee of them.

THE NATIONS

As their creator, Yahweh is sovereign in relation to the nations. That fact lies behind his appointing Jeremiah "over the nations, over the kingdoms." He is summoning them to "come and put each one his throne at the opening of Jerusalem's gateways" (Jer 1:10, 15). If he is thus acting against Judah's wrongdoing, how could he not act against the other nations themselves? Thus,

> Yahweh roars from on high,
> > from his sacred dwelling he gives voice,
> > he roars and roars against his abode.
> He chants a cry like grape-treaders
> > to all earth's inhabitants.
> The din has come to the end of the earth,
> > because Yahweh has an argument for the nations.
> He's entering into judgment with all flesh;
> > the faithless—he's giving them to the sword. (Jer 25:30-31)

Yet for the nations, as for Israel, it is not his last word.

> About all my neighbors who deal badly, who touch the domain that I gave to my people Israel: here am I, I'm going to uproot them from on their land, and Judah's household I shall uproot from among them. But after I've uprooted them I shall again show compassion to them and bring them back, each to his domain, each to his country. If they really learn the ways of my people, swearing

by my name "As Yahweh lives" as they taught my people to swear by the Master, they'll be built up among my people. But if they don't listen, I'll uproot that nation, uproot and destroy it. (Jer 12:14-17)

The neighbors who live near Yahweh's domain are peoples such as Moab, Edom, and Ammon, who are not Judah's big aggressor but are happy to join in with Babylon in attacking the land that Yahweh viewed as his domain. Like Babylon, they will not get away with their aggression, even though they unconsciously undertake it as Yahweh's agents. As Yahweh uproots Judah from its land (it was the first verb Yahweh used back in Jer 1:10), so he will uproot them. But then uprooting becomes a positive image. Precisely because they were Judah's neighbors, such peoples were natural places for Judahites to take refuge when the imperial power invaded. So as well as bringing Judahites back from Babylon, Yahweh will "uproot" Judahites from there. There are more surprises. For Judah planting is to follow uprooting. While not using that image for his neighbors, Yahweh says something equivalent. For the first time, the Jeremiah scroll talks about Yahweh having "compassion," a word related to the term for a mother's womb. Yahweh has a mother's feelings for . . . Moab, Edom, and Ammon. He will bring each back to its domain. Again "bring back" is a telling verb, the expression Yahweh uses for bringing the Judahites back from exile.

There is yet more, though there is a kick in the tail. Yahweh envisages that these peoples will "learn the ways of my people," with the specific implication of "swearing by my name" as opposed to swearing by the Master as they taught the Israelites to do (Yahweh speaks loosely, since "the Master" was strictly the Canaanites' deity rather than these neighbors' god). Swearing by Yahweh's name is a synecdoche for recognizing Yahweh as the real God. These neighbors will be "built up" in Israel's midst—Yahweh picks up another expression from his commission of Jeremiah, where "building up" was one of the antitheses of "uprooting," to describe Judah's destiny. "Building up" too will apply to the people who were once the agents of pulling down (Jer 1:10), though only if they listen to this expectation of Yahweh's— otherwise they too will be "uprooted" and "destroyed" (that verb came in Jer 1:10 too).

En passant, Jeremiah earlier made the point in another concrete way that provokes the imagination. He was talking about "the ark of the covenant," the chest that contained the document with the terms of the pledge between

Yahweh and Israel. At some stage it disappears from Israel's story; it was presumably destroyed or taken as plunder (hence the "lost ark," as in *Raiders of the Lost Ark*). The loss would be devastating. Actually, Jeremiah says, "It won't come to mind, they won't be mindful of it or give attention; it won't be made again." The reason is that "at that time they'll call Jerusalem 'Yahweh's throne.'" And when Jerusalem is reestablished as Yahweh's throne, "all the nations will gather to it, to Yahweh's name" (Jer 3:16-17). The promise contains the opposite of a sting in the tail. The restoration of Jerusalem and Judah will attract not merely Judahites from all over the world, and Ephraimites from all over the world and all over the country, but "all the nations," in keeping with a vision such as the one in Isaiah 2:2-4. To put it another way, if Israel comes back to Yahweh and swears,

> "As Yahweh lives,"
>> in truth and in the faithful exercise of authority,
> Nations will pray to be blessed by him,
>> and will exult in him. (Jer 4:2)

Talk of nations praying to be blessed comes otherwise only in Genesis 22:18; 26:4; Psalm 72:17. The vision associated with Yahweh's promise to Abraham will find fulfillment.

OTHER FAITHS

Yahweh is the only God. Jeremiah draws attention to two contexts that require Judah to sort out its attitude to other faiths—Canaan and Babylon. (Egypt, where Jeremiah 39–44 indicates that some Judahites end up, would be another such context, but Jeremiah does not refer to the issue there.)

Jeremiah 10:1-16 is the Jeremiah scroll's systematic reflection on Babylonian religion set against the background of the first forced migration of Judahites to Babylon in 597. It presupposes and derides two impressive aspects of Babylonian religion: its sophisticated, wide-ranging reflection on the created world, the planets and the stars, their relationship to events in the world, and their influence on events; and its impressive statues of gods, which were carried around in processions that the exiles might witness. First,

> Don't learn the nations' way;
>> don't shatter at signs in the heavens.
> Because the nations may shatter at those,
>> because the peoples' laws are hollow. (Jer 10:2-3)

The planets' movements can seem to bode something worrying to the Babylonians; hence the multiplicity of their attempts to understand them, so as to control their own destiny. But their understanding of the rules by which the world operates is hollow. While there are rules whereby the cosmos works (see "The Creator's World" earlier in this chapter), they are not the rules that the Babylonians identify.

Second, there are those impressive images, overlaid with silver and gold, clothed in blue and purple. But think about how they come into existence, Jeremiah says. Someone has to fell a tree before the nice column gets overlaid, they have to fasten it down so it doesn't wobble, and they have to carry it because it can't walk; nor can it speak, nor can it actually do anything (good or bad). These wooden "gods" are also hollow, empty (*hebel*), as evanescent or insubstantial as a breath (Jeremiah likes this word—cf. Jer 2:5; 8:19; 14:22; 16:19; 51:18). There is no reason to be "in awe of them." It ought to be obvious. Really "every goldsmith is put to shame by his image." In this connection, "every human being proves stupid, without knowledge" (Jer 10:14).

The pathetic nature of Babylonian theology and worship contrasts with what Israel knows about Yahweh.

> There is none like you, Yahweh;
>> you are great and your name is great, with strength.
> Who would not be in awe of you, king of the nations,
>> because it's fitting to you.
> Because among all the nations' smart people
>> and in all their dominion there's none like you. (Jer 10:6-7)

A decisive difference between God and the gods is that the gods can die and will die.

> Yahweh is the true God,
>> he's the living God, the everlasting King. . . .
> The gods that didn't make the heavens and the earth
>> will perish from the earth and from under the heavens. (Jer 10:10, 11)

It's in that context that Jeremiah refers to Yahweh's being the real God who made the earth by his energy and established it by his expertise (Jer 10:12-13; see chap. 5 above). He describes the objects of Babylonian worship:

> They're hollow, a work for mockery;
>> at the time when they're attended to, they'll perish.

Not like these is Jacob's share,
because he's the one who formed everything. (Jer 10:15-16)

Babylonian religion knew that the statues simply represented the gods. They were not identical with them; the gods were invisible supernatural figures. It's really the statues that will perish. But Jeremiah ignores this theological nuance, which was perhaps not in the front of the mind of the average Babylonian, or the average Judahite living in Babylon. In due course the statues were going to be smashed and burned, and this fate would mirror the fate of the entities they represented, because they do not have life residing in them as Yahweh does. They are created beings; they come into existence and they can die.

MEMBERS OF OTHER NATIONS

Whereas the nations have good reason to worry when they see foreboding signs in the heavens, Israel has no reason. Israelites ought to know better. If only they would recognize that

what comes from the hills belongs to falsehood,
the uproar from the mountains. (Jer 3:23)

The nations need to know better too. They are destined to seek Yahweh's blessing, and this seeking will involve acknowledging the one God and the emptiness of their so-called gods.

Yahweh, my vigor and my stronghold,
my escape in the day of pressure,
To you nations will come
from earth's ends and say,
"Our ancestors indeed had falsehood as their domain,
hollowness, and there was nothing in them that would prevail.
Can a human being make himself gods?–
but they're not gods."
Therefore here am I, I'm going to make them acknowledge it
at this moment.
I shall make them acknowledge my hand and my strength,
and they will acknowledge that my name is Yahweh. (Jer 16:19-21)

In a post-modern context, Christians need to keep affirming to themselves and to others that the story of Yahweh's involvement with Israel (in which Jeremiah has a central place), which leads into the story of Jesus, is key to an understanding of God and of the world, while recognizing our vocation to accept the adherents of other faiths amongst whom we live and to be concerned for their well-being. Jeremiah suggests this point in a letter to those victims of forced migration in 597.

> Yahweh of Armies, Israel's God, has said this to the entire exile community that I exiled from Jerusalem to Babylon. "Build houses and live, plant gardens and eat their fruit. Take wives and have sons and daughters, take wives for your sons and give your daughters to husbands, so they may have sons and daughters. Become many there; don't become few. Seek the well-being of the city where I've exiled you; plead on its behalf with Yahweh, because in its well-being there will be well-being for you." (Jer 29:4-7)

There is a difference between the position of these people Jeremiah is writing to and (say) people in the United States or Europe receiving migrants from Syria or Libya. The Judahites were the migrants, and Jeremiah is talking about the foreign people that they had to live among. And he wants people to take a positive attitude to these foreign people because he knows that the Judahites need to settle down to an exile that will last decades not months. The stance he commends is nevertheless instructive, especially when combined with his strictness of attitude to the Babylonians' faith. The Judahites are to seek the well-being of the city where they live. The concrete expression of this seeking that he mentions is their praying for their Babylonian neighbors. He doesn't mention witnessing to them, arguing with them, or seeking to convert them, though the message about other nations in Jeremiah 12 (quoted in "The Nations" earlier in this chapter) indicates that such conversion is something Yahweh is interested in. The Judahites are to avoid being attracted by their faith and to look forward to the time when Yahweh opens their eyes.

GOD IN CHRISTIAN THEOLOGY

Systematic theology classically affirms that God is one, and is omnipotent, omniscient, omnipresent, eternal, self-sufficient, immutable, and impassible. How would Jeremiah relate to these descriptions?

- God is one: and it's crucial to Jeremiah that Yahweh is the one and only God. Jeremiah's faith is monotheistic. There are two ways in which Jeremiah might want to nuance that statement. First, for him the important question is who is God, not merely how many gods there are. The faith of someone like Jeremiah can thus be called "mono-Yahwistic." The implication is not that this theological conviction is less advanced or less sophisticated than a monotheistic formulation—if anything, the opposite is the case. Yahweh's being the one God is at least as important as the fact that there is only God. Second, Jeremiah recognizes that there are lots of gods even though there is only one God. There are lots of supernatural beings created by God and vulnerable to having their lives ended by God, beings who are created to be God's supernatural agents in the world, though there is only one God, Yahweh.

- God is omnipotent: Jeremiah would affirm that Yahweh has the power to do anything, though he doesn't use that power very much. He doesn't force Judah to act in the way he wishes. But he is the "big strong man God (Yahweh is his name), big in counsel and mighty in deed" (Jer 32:18-19).

- God is omniscient: Jeremiah would affirm that Yahweh has the capacity to know whatever he wants to know. There is no deceiving of Yahweh and no hiding from Yahweh (Jer 23:23-24). But his knowing involves an active discovering, not simply a passive possessing of a knowledge bank: "Yes, I myself, I've been looking" (Jer 7:11; cf. Jer 20:12; 32:19, 24). And paradoxically, he can un-know: "their wrongdoing I shall not keep in mind any more" (Jer 31:34).

- God is omnipresent: Jeremiah would affirm that Yahweh can be wherever he wants to be, though he also suggests nuances in the idea of Yahweh's presence. There is a difference between his general presence in the world and his presence in the temple, and the idea of Yahweh being "with" you is different again. Yahweh can throw people out of his presence (Jer 7:15; 15:1; 52:3) and he can abandon them (Jer 12:7).

- God is eternal: Jeremiah would affirm that there has never been a time when Yahweh was not and that there will never be a time when he is not. Yahweh is the true God, the living God, the everlasting king (Jer 10:10). "Living God" is a key description (Jer 4:2; 5:2; 12:16; 16:14, 15; 22:24; 23:7, 8, 36; 38:16; 44:26). He has lived and will live through all time. But he lives in time with his people and his world. He is unconstrained by time rather than timeless or outside time.

- God is self-sufficient: Jeremiah would affirm that Yahweh has life in himself—his being does not derive from elsewhere.

- God is immutable: Jeremiah would affirm that Yahweh is consistent and in this sense is not changeable, though he is flexible in relation to people's relationship with him. Jeremiah is explicit on Yahweh's willingness to relent or have a change of heart in response to people (Jer 18:1-10; see "Jeremiah 18–20 Begins: Think About God's Sovereignty" in chap. 3 above); Jeremiah is not worried that God's changing his mind might compromise his omniscience.

- God is impassible: Jeremiah would affirm that Yahweh is not irrationally or uncontrollably or unpredictably emotional, but he emphasizes Yahweh's capacity for joy, anger, disappointment, and grief. He also speaks of God's pain at his people's suffering: "My insides moan for him, I have deep compassion for him (Yahweh's declaration)" (Jer 31:20). But it's hard to be sure when Jeremiah is talking about his own pain and when of Yahweh's.

It is Jeremiah's God who is incarnate in Jesus. Jesus does not claim to reveal anything new about God's character and neither does the New Testament say he revealed anything new about it. What Jesus did was embody, before people's eyes, the God of whom Jeremiah and the rest of the Scriptures spoke (and in the process generate a new revelation of God's person as three-in-one). While Jeremiah puts more emphasis on God's anger and redress than (e.g.) Isaiah, he talks of wrath less than Romans or Revelation do (see "The Future in Christian Theology" in chap. 8 below). Jesus' warnings about weeping and gnashing of teeth and of the temple's destruction parallel Jeremiah's warnings, and Jesus quotes Yahweh's severe critique of Judah in Jeremiah 7 when he throws people out of the temple (Mt 21:12-13).

The tough side to Yahweh and to Jesus makes Christians uncomfortable (so we slide over the tough side to Jesus). Jeremiah makes it difficult to avoid. On the other hand, we should also note that Jeremiah does not imply—for instance—that Yahweh's violence gives us the excuse for violence. If anything, the opposite is true. Like the Psalms, Jeremiah entrusts the violence to Yahweh.

CHAPTER SIX

THE PEOPLE OF GOD

Yahweh is Israel's God and Israel is Yahweh's people.
While Yahweh is the creator and lord of the entire world, within that world
Israel is "my people." Jeremiah does not discuss why it should be so or how it
came to be so; the question is, will it always be so? But who or what is this Israel?

A Possession, a Household, a Community

The images for understanding Israel come from its life, like the images for understanding God, such as master, teacher, and husband. As a "people" (*'am*), Israel
is a community bound together by quasi-familial ties. It is a kind of hugely
extended family. "Israel's household" (Jer 48:13) comprises a collection of clans
descended from one ancestor, Jacob. The clans comprised many kin-groups, but
the northern clans had split off from Judah after Solomon's reign, so that northern
Israel or Ephraim constituted one nation and Judah constituted another. Jeremiah doesn't seem troubled by this split (three centuries ago) as a generator of
disunity, though he is troubled by it because it also meant the northern clans
abandoning faithfulness to Yahweh. As a result, Yahweh had abandoned Ephraim
to Assyrian conquest and exile a century previously, and Judah ought surely to
be concerned about Yahweh's throwing out its "brothers" from their land
(Jer 7:15). Jeremiah promises that Yahweh hasn't abandoned the northern clans.

Being family ought to make a difference to the way people treat each other.
The family is a key part of the community safety net (see "Jeremiah 34–36

Begins: Think About What Is Written" in chap. 4 above). It means people relate to each other as brothers and sisters (Jer 34:9, 14, 17; Jeremiah is picking up the Torah's argument that the Israelite community should treat one another as family). Whereas family members might care for one another but not relate to the people next door, they are actually to resist the idea that "an Englishman's home is his castle." In terms of a different image, the community is to treat needy people as neighbors (Jer 34:15, 17), taking steps to ensure that individuals get along with their neighbors (Jer 7:5). As a king should regard fellow Israelites as his brothers and sisters (Deut 17:14-20), so he should regard and treat them as neighbors (Jer 22:13)—which in Jerusalem they literally are. It's thus scandalous when people can't rely on their brothers or their neighbors (Jer 9:4-5) and when within the local community men are engaged in adultery with their neighbors' wives (Jer 5:8; 29:23).

More metaphorically, Israel is the "domain" that belongs to Yahweh—as Yahweh is Israel's "share" (Jer 10:16; cf. Jer 51:19). A family has a stretch of land that belongs to it, its domain, which is the basis of its livelihood. Nobody can trespass on a family's right to live on this land and work it. While Yahweh refers to Canaan as "my domain," he also uses that expression more metaphorically of Israel. Yahweh especially claims Israel, and it is thus sacred to Yahweh, like the first fruits of the harvest (Jer 2:3), and like Jeremiah himself, and like the Sabbath each week, which is Yahweh's day. It means people mustn't trespass on it. Etymologically the word for "domain" (*nahalah*) denotes something that was inherited, but Yahweh of course doesn't inherit things from anyone, and the word's connotation in practice is more that it is something of which one is in indisputable control.

Given that Israel is Yahweh's domain, his inalienable possession, it's extraordinary and scandalous that Yahweh says,

I have abandoned my household,
    I have deserted my domain.
I have given my dearly beloved
    into her enemies' fist.
My domain has become to me
    like a lion in the forest.
She's given her voice against me;
    therefore I've been hostile to her.
My domain is a colored bird of prey;
    birds of prey are against her, all round.

Go, gather all the creatures of the wild,
  bring them to eat. (Jer 12:7-9)

A COUNTRY, A DOMAIN

The image of a domain does apply to the country as well as the people. Yahweh sees Canaan as "a desirable country, the most splendid domain of the nations"; it belongs to him and he is therefore in a position to give it to Israel (Jer 3:19). He says, "all my neighbors who deal badly, who touch the domain that I gave to my people Israel: here am I, I'm going to uproot them from on their land" (Jer 12:14). The neighbors are people such as Moab, Edom, and Ammon, but the same will hold for Babylon:

The Chaldeans will become spoil;
  all its despoilers will be full (Yahweh's declaration),
Because you rejoice, because you exult,
  plunderers of my domain,
Because you jump like a heifer with grain;
  you bellow like sturdy ones. (Jer 50:10-11)

But again scandalously, Yahweh has to say to Judah itself:

I enabled you to come into a country of farmland,
  to eat its fruit and its good things.
But you came and defiled my country;
  you made my domain something offensive. (Jer 2:7)

Therefore, Judah will pay a price analogous to that with which Yahweh threatened the peoples around:

You'll forfeit hold (and by your own act)
  of your domain that I gave you.
I shall make you serve your enemies
  in a country that you haven't known. (Jer 17:4)

But it won't be the end of the story. "I shall hurl you from upon this country to a country that you haven't known, you or your ancestors." But later, "days are coming (Yahweh's affirmation) when it will no more be said, 'Yahweh is alive, who got the Israelites up from the country of Egypt,' but rather, 'Yahweh is alive who got the Israelites up from the northern country and from all the countries where he drove them away.' I will return them to their land that I gave to their ancestors" (Jer 16:13-15).

The Jeremiah scroll includes a vivid and concrete narrative about the country in Jeremiah's account of his claiming possession on his family's behalf of a stretch of their land in Anathoth. Possibly the family had lost possession of the land, perhaps through economic difficulties and debt, and Jeremiah is under pressure to use his resources to reestablish its possession (Jer 32:7-8). In other words, he is to undertake an act of "restoration" or "redemption" (*ge'ullah*) in respect of the "possession" (*yerushshah*)—that noun comes from the verb regularly used of Israel's entering into possession of the land of Canaan. Jeremiah did so and got his associate Baruch to see to the proper sealing of the relevant documents: "'put them in an earthen container so that they may stand for a long time.' Because Yahweh of Armies, Israel's God, has said this: 'Houses, fields, and vineyards will again be acquired in this country'" (Jer 32:13-15).

A CITY AND ITS SABBATH

Cities were not part of God's vision from the beginning. The original city was the idea of Cain or his son (Gen 4:17; the sentence is ambiguous). The original Jerusalem was David's idea, but Yahweh adopted it and got enthusiastic about it. Being more of a country boy doesn't stop Jeremiah enthusing about Jerusalem, though not like Isaiah and the Psalms. But in Jeremiah, Jerusalem is not "the holy city" or "the city of God." The city does appear right at the beginning of the Jeremiah scroll as an image for Jeremiah's own security: "I am making you into a fortified city" (Jer 1:18). But Jeremiah's references to the present city of Jerusalem and the other towns in Judah are overwhelmingly negative; the city is a place where wrongdoing thrives. Yet Yahweh's ultimate intention for Jerusalem and the other towns is that they should flourish. "The city will be built up for Yahweh from the Hanan'el Tower to the Corner Gate, and the measuring line will go out again straight to Gareb Hill and turn to Go'ah. The entire vale (corpses and ashes) and all the open country as far as Wadi Kidron and as far as the Horses Gate on the east will be sacred for Yahweh. It won't be uprooted or torn down again ever" (Jer 31:38-40). For Yahweh,

> "It will mean a name to celebrate, and praise and splendor, to all the nations of the earth that hear of all the good things that I'm going to do with them, and they will be in awe and will shiver because of all the good things and all the well-being that I'm going to do for it."

Yahweh has said this: "A voice will make itself heard in this place, . . . the voice of joy and of celebration, the voice of groom and of bride, the voice of people saying, 'Confess Yahweh of Armies, because Yahweh is good, because his commitment lasts permanently,' bringing a thank-offering to Yahweh's house." (Jer 33:9-11)

Jerusalem will become the place from which Yahweh will rule the world; it is destined to be seen by the world as Yahweh's throne (Jer 3:16-17).

While the relationship of city and country can be tricky (see "Jeremiah 30–33 Begins: Think About Restoration and Returning" in chap. 4 above), the two need each other. The Sabbath symbolizes an aspect of this tension. Broadly, the Ten Commandments concern themselves with prohibiting things that people incline to and requiring things that people do not. For modern observant Jews the Sabbath is a delight, but for ancient Israelites it was often a nuisance. Yahweh bids Jeremiah stand in a gateway through which Judahite kings came into the city and proclaim to Judahites in general that they should not carry loads through the city's gateways on the Sabbath or take out loads from the houses on the Sabbath (Jer 17:19-27). It's a longstanding expectation, he says. Actually, the Ten Commandments say nothing about carrying a load. The commandments go back to a time when there was no big city like Jerusalem and no trade; what Sabbath observance meant was no plowing and no harvesting. But Israel has developed, and there is now trade between city and country in farm produce and in wares such as pottery and metalwork, in which craftworkers engaged in their homes in the city. So "work" includes activities related to this new socioeconomic context. And Yahweh still expects Judah to "make the Sabbath day sacred" by not engaging in activities related to this work. He says nothing about people needing a rest on the Sabbath. The point about the Sabbath is that Yahweh claims this day as a sign that really all time belongs to him. "Give me this day, and you can decide what to do on the other days." The logic resembles that for tithes: "give me a tenth in recognition that all your produce comes from me, and you can keep the rest." It's a hard demand. Give up trade for a day—the day when people have most leisure time to buy things? Yes, that's the point, Yahweh implies. You want to be able to enjoy the festivals when people come through these gateways from all over the country to celebrate Passover, Pentecost, and Sukkot? Keep the Sabbath in the city each week then.

A city is indeed designed to be a place that offers security, and it therefore risks being a temptation. Jerusalem could bring that temptation, cleverly located as it was, surrounded on three sides by canyons. Yahweh warns it about such a dynamic (Jer 21:13). For all his commitment to Jerusalem, he speaks often of giving it into the hand of the king of Babylon (Jer 32:3, 24, 25, 28) and declares, "I've hidden my face from this city" (Jer 33:5). But that hiding will not be the end:

> Here am I, I'm going to restore the fortunes of Jacob's tents,
>> and on his dwellings I shall have compassion.
> A city will be built on its tell;
>> a citadel will sit on its authorized place.
> Thanksgiving will go out from them,
>> and the sound of people having fun.
> I shall make them many and they won't become few;
>> I shall make them honourable and they won't become small.
> Its children will be as of old,
>> its assembly will stand established before me,
>> and I shall attend to all its oppressors.
> Its august one will come from within it
>> and its ruler will go out from within it.
> I shall draw it near and it will come up to me,
>> because who is the one
>> who would have pledged his own mind to come up to me (Yahweh's
>>> declaration)?
> So you will be a people for me
>> and I shall be God for you. (Jer 30:18-22)

WELL-BEING

One could say, then, that Yahweh has a vision of well-being (*shalom*) for Jerusalem. We don't know whether there is an etymological link between the city's name, *Yerushalayim*, and the word *shalom*. But it seems likely that people in Jerusalem would make a link. In modern Hebrew *shalom* is a greeting like "hello," and people may not think about its meaning, though it half-implies, "Hi, how are you, I hope things are well." That connotation is not far from the word's implications in Jeremiah as elsewhere in the First Testament. There is overlap between *shalom* and "peace," the traditional default English translation of the word, but only overlap. In just one or two passages, Jeremiah uses *shalom* to denote peace as opposed to war or conflict.

> With his mouth someone speaks with his neighbour of shalom,
>> but inside he lays an ambush for him. (Jer 9:8)

Another passage promises a king that he will die in shalom not in wartime (Jer 34:5).

Nor does *shalom* denote inner peace, peace of mind. Jeremiah believes in inner peace, but *shalom* wouldn't be his word for it. He uses the negative-sounding expression "don't be afraid" (e.g., Jer 1:8; 10:5; 30:10; 46:27-28), which might not sound like much, just the absence of a negative, but it is a big encouragement in the Scriptures. More positively, he talks about a true security that issues a sense of security (Jer 23:6; 32:37; 33:16; contrast the false sense of security to which Jer 49:31 refers).

While shalom thus includes absence of conflict and would imply a sense of security, it suggests a bigger fullness of life. Jeremiah uses the word when he urges Judahites to "seek the shalom of the city where I've exiled you; plead on its behalf with Yahweh, because in its shalom there will be shalom for you" (see "Members of Other Nations" in chap. 5 above). The overlap between *shalom* and the name of the people's home city might add piquancy to Jeremiah's exhortation; he is almost saying, make your Babylonian home into a new Jerusalem. Jeremiah has just urged Judahites in Babylon to "build houses and live, plant gardens and eat their fruit. Take wives and have sons and daughters, take wives for your sons and give your daughters to husbands, so they may have sons and daughters. Become many there; don't become few" (Jer 29:4-7). It would make sense if shalom at least included these realities. So it is when Yahweh makes promises about shalom back in Jerusalem (Jer 33:6-9). In both contexts, shalom has a wide range. It covers both the material and the spiritual, both people's lives in the world and their lives in relation to God. It's possible to think that God's main concern is with people's lives in relation to him and that material things don't matter too much; the material, this-worldly aspect to shalom confronts that idea. It's also possible to think that happy family life, good food, and satisfying work are what constitutes shalom; that idea is also too narrow.

The big problem about shalom-talk in Jeremiah doesn't involve either of those false antitheses. Jerusalemites knew that shalom involved both worldly life and worship. But they were serving false deities instead of Yahweh or relying on unfaithfulness in their worldly relationships. And their priests and prophets were colluding with this false understanding of shalom.

> Don't listen to the words of the prophets
> who prophesy to you.

They're giving you something hollow;
>> they speak a vision from their mind,
>> not from Yahweh's mouth.
They're saying to people who disdain Yahweh's word,
>> "There will be shalom for you."
To everyone who's walking by the determination of his mind,
>> they've said, "Bad fortune won't come upon you." (Jer 23:16-17; cf. Jer 6:14)

The problem with the people we call false prophets is that they were shalom prophets (see "Jeremiah 26–29 Begins: Think About the Reassuring Prophets" in chap. 4 above), promising shalom when shalom was incompatible with the city's moral and religious stance.

LEADERS

Nearly all the time Yahweh works through people, not directly. One could guess about the reasons, but the Scriptures don't. Likewise, Jeremiah takes for granted forms of leadership that Israel takes for granted—kings, priests, experts, and prophets. As is the case with the rationale for Yahweh's special relationship with Israel, he doesn't discuss whether there should be kings, priests, experts, and prophets. Other peoples had them; Israel has them. Elsewhere the First Testament hints at rationales. One reason Israel had kings is that without them everybody did as they liked and it produced moral and social chaos (Judg 21:25). One reason Israel had priests is that they could be responsible for knowing Yahweh's expectations of people and for teaching people about them, for ensuring that people were not too casual in their approach to God, and for safeguarding Yahweh's holiness (Deut 33:8-11). One reason Israel had experts, counselors, and advisers was that somebody had to bear the burden of sorting out disputes and questions in the community (Ex 18:13-26). One reason Israel had prophets was that Yahweh needed to intervene to confront people about what was going on (Judg 6:7-10 is the first occasion), all the more when Israel had kings who were in a position to make up their own minds about political questions or were under pressure to do so. All the forms of leadership can be a blessing. In Jeremiah's day, all look more like a curse.

Explore Jerusalem's streets, please look, and get to know,
>> seek in its squares, if you can find anyone,
If there's someone exercising authority
>> seeking truthfulness. (Jer 5:1)

What he articulates about the experts, the smart people, he would wish applied to all of them:

> The smart person isn't to exult in his smartness,
>> the strong person isn't to exult in his strength,
>> the wealthy person isn't to exult in his wealth.
> Rather the person who exults is to exult in this:
>> showing insight and acknowledging me,
> That I am Yahweh,
>> acting with commitment,
> With authority and faithfulness in the country,
>> because I delight in these things. (Jer 9:23-24)

Such acknowledgment of Yahweh is the key background quality for priests and prophets. The trouble is,

> The priests didn't say "Where is Yahweh?"
>> the people controlling the instruction didn't acknowledge me.
> The shepherds rebelled against me,
>> the prophets prophesied by the Master,
>> and followed beings that couldn't prevail in anything. (Jer 2:8)

Asking "Where is Yahweh" is a key way of acknowledging Yahweh. And controlling the instruction is a frightening description of being in a position to mislead people. The priests and prophets determine the teaching that people receive. It is as if they are the people who decide which Scriptures are read in church. Jeremiah's critique takes us back to shalom. By the way they exercise their power, they determine how people understand shalom, how they understand the life of the country and the city, and how they understand both Yahweh's expectations and Yahweh's promises.

THE PEOPLE OF GOD IN CHRISTIAN THEOLOGY

Christian thinking can assume that God relates primarily to the individual believer. Jeremiah would find this assumption puzzling. He takes for granted God's entering into a relationship with a family that would become a great people, though he does also assume the reality of the individual's relationship with God and responsibility to God. He imagines looking around Jerusalem to investigate individuals, and he urges the individual to exult in acknowledging Yahweh and not in smartness, energy, or resources (Jer 5:1-5; 9:23-24). But he maintains a dynamic relationship between being part of a community and being an individual.

Christian thinking emphasizes the importance of the leadership of the church, though that emphasis takes different forms in different contexts. Parts of the church have thought that having bishops and priests (with a historical link to the apostles) was essential to the church's being, so that the church didn't really exist if it had no such bishops and priests. Much of the church assumes it is natural to have one person as a chief or sole pastor of a congregation. Much of the church assumes that thinking hard about leadership is of key importance. Jeremiah would be puzzled by these assumptions. He emphasizes the sinfulness of the people of God's leadership and suggests criteria for evaluating leadership that focus on faithfulness to God and to people.

To combine the words of Mary, Zechariah, and Simeon, "Jesus came to the aid of his servant Israel" so that "being rescued from the hand of our enemies we [members of Israel] might serve him" and he might bring "a light for revelation to nations" (Lk 1:54, 74; 2:32). It worked only partially. As happened in Jeremiah's day, only a "remainder" of Israel came through the event of Jesus' coming successfully (Rom 11:5), though the Gentile aspect of the aim worked better. But the body that did recognize Jesus came to be so dominated by Gentiles that it forgot its origin as an extension of Israel or as a vast expansion of that remainder. Within Christian theology, one might then distinguish a number of positions regarding the significance of Israel. For example:

- the church replaced Israel in God's purpose
- the Jewish people relates to God on the basis of his covenant with them and the church relates to God on the basis of the new covenant made through Jesus
- God no longer works with a national Israel but continues to be committed to the Jewish people and intends that it should recognize Jesus as Messiah
- the real question is how Israel relates to the Palestinians in the traditional bounds of the promised land

How might Jeremiah relate to these alternatives?

- Jeremiah speaks with more than one voice about Israel's security or vulnerability. He speaks of God annihilating Israel, of his decimating Israel but preserving a small community, and of his restoring Israel and vastly increasing its numbers. Jeremiah does not seek to reconcile these different positions in the way Paul does in Romans 9–11. Maybe he was glad when he could eventually read Romans—or will be when he gets the chance.

- The new covenant could solve the problem reflected in that ambiguity. Fulfilling the new covenant promise would mean that Israel would not be unfaithful to Yahweh anymore, so there wouldn't be a need to cut Israel down. The logic means the new covenant does need to be fulfilled for Jews and not just for Gentiles. A new covenant that turned out chiefly to benefit Gentiles would deconstruct. It would lose its point.

- The idea of there being a people of Israel that lacked a land and a national identity would also not make sense to Jeremiah. But neither would a people of Israel that marginalized or subjugated or harassed other people in its midst. A renewed Israel that got its land and national identity back would need to be an Israel that was faithful to God and a blessing to other peoples.

CHAPTER SEVEN

WRONGDOING

LIKE MOST PROPHETS, Jeremiah was commissioned to confront Israel about its wrongdoings and warn it about the consequences that would follow from them. There are a number of aspects to these wrongdoings, and Jeremiah has a number of images for them. In relation to God, they involve unfaithfulness, rebellion, and waywardness, and they issue in taint and shame.

UNFAITHFULNESS, REBELLION, WAYWARDNESS, TRANSGRESSION, HEEDLESSNESS

In outlining his commission to Jeremiah, Yahweh declares:

> I shall speak my rulings to them,
> for all their bad dealing, in that they've abandoned me.
> They've burned incense to other gods,
> bowed low to things their hands made. (Jer 1:16)

The arraignment of Judah that fills out this charge (Jer 2:1-13) starts from the strange clash between Israel's initial commitment and its speedy turning away. Having been initially dedicated to its marriage to Yahweh, it then turned to another protector and provider, the Master (*ba'al*). Ironically, the title of this other deity means "husband" in a patriarchal sense (it's not the First Testament's regular word for talking about husbands and wives—the usual ones are the ordinary words for woman and man, so that "his wife" and "her husband" is more literally "his woman" and "her man"). Turning to other deities is analogous to adultery in marriage; put more sharply, it's equivalent to whoring (Jer 3:1-20). Israel expressed its initial faithfulness to Yahweh by trusting him for what it needed on the wilderness journey. In Canaan, it looked elsewhere. It needed rain so the crops could grow. It needed its women-folk to be able to have children. People wanted to know what the future might hold and needed protection from adversaries. Inexplicably, Israel looked to other gods or to more powerful political allies to provide what it needed. Its unfaithfulness thus expressed itself in political policy making and in community worship (controlled by the men) and family worship (over which the woman had more influence; see Jer 44:15-25). Jeremiah doesn't always distinguish clearly between looking to other gods and looking to po-litical allies as ways of being faithless; both are false forms of reliance, ways of being untrue by not looking to Yahweh. To use a political image, they are equivalent to breaking faith, to treachery.

As well as husband, Yahweh is master, king, director, teacher, and creator. Israel's wrongdoing thus also involves rebellion, waywardness, and heed-lessness. Yahweh is a farmer working with his oxen, but the oxen have re-fused to submit themselves to the authority of his yoke in order to serve him; they have broken their straps (Jer 2:19-20; 5:5). Israel has called on God as father and guide (Jer 3:4) but has not behaved like an obedient child or a responsive pupil. Yahweh is king and Israel has defied him and rebelled against him (Jer 2:29; 4:17; 5:23). Yahweh pointed Israel toward a path, but it chose different paths (Jer 2:17-18, 23, 25, 33, 36; 4:18). Yahweh had urged it to think again about its path and about the ancient paths, but it had re-fused (Jer 6:16). It was deliberately wayward (Jer 2:22; 3:13, 21; 5:25). And it was living in denial (Jer 2:34-35).

The prophets' words and the priests' instruction have the same content and the same authority. They are mutually supportive. It is by paying heed to them that people could fulfill the expectation to which Yahweh referred when he said, "Listen to my voice, and I will become God for you and you will become a people for me; and go by the entire path that I order you so that it may be good for you" (Jer 7:23). Instead, "they abandoned my instruction which I put before them. They didn't listen to my voice and they didn't walk by it. They followed the de-termination of their mind and followed the Masters, as their ancestors taught them" (Jer 9:13-14). They have eyes and ears but they don't use them, and they willfully mislead themselves about the cause of their problems (Jer 5:21-25).

Taint, Corruption, Profanation

Israel's unfaithfulness and waywardness has tainted the country. Yahweh brought Israel into a land that especially belonged to him, but it has worshiped the Master there and thereby defiled it (Jer 2:7). ·

The idea of cleanness and defilement presupposes that some things are compatible with who Yahweh is and some are incompatible. Things that are whole or alive or upright or matching Yahweh in other ways are clean. Things that are compromised in their unity (such as animals that have unusual combinations of features), that are dead, and that are wayward do not fit with who Yahweh is; the same applies to the realm of sex, because Yahweh is not a sexual being. Such things convey defilement and make a person taboo, and people or places that have been in contact with them need to have their cleanness or purity restored if Yahweh is to associate with them. Worshiping other deities is a way Israel has brought defilement onto Yahweh's own country. Israel has made the country something offensive or abhorrent, something that in its nature is alien to who Yahweh is and clashes with what he therefore accepts (Jer 16:18). These words are strongly affective.

People have even defiled the temple with offensive things.

> They put their abominations in the house over which my name has been called out, to defile it, and they built up the shrines of the Master in the Ben-hinnom Ravine to make their sons and their daughters pass through the fire to the Shameful King, which I didn't order them (it didn't come into my mind), to do this offensive thing, so as to cause Judah to do wrong. (Jer 32:34-35; cf. 7:30-31)

> They've abandoned me, made this place alien, burned sacrifices in it to other gods that they hadn't acknowledged, they, their ancestors, and Judah's kings. They've filled this place with the blood of people free of guilt. (Jer 19:4)

Their abandonment and defilement can involve overt prayer to other deities. But it can also involve prayer that is formally addressed to Yahweh who is conceived in such a Master-like way that it is really prayer to the Master even if people don't acknowledge it. People offer children as sacrifices to Yahweh in connection with their prayers, but a Yahweh conceived as welcoming such sacrifices is not Yahweh at all. Jeremiah's references to shedding the blood of needy people who are free of guilt also might cover the killing of prophets (e.g., Jer 26:20-23). It might cover fraud that had that result or failure to exercise authority in a way that protected innocent people. People involved in such action or neglect might attempt to exonerate themselves by saying that actually they had done nothing (exactly, one might retort). When they made promises in Yahweh's name and then broke them, they profaned Yahweh's name (Jer 34:12-16). Their wrongdoing taints the people themselves as well as the land.

> If you wash with soap
>   and use much detergent for yourself,
>   your waywardness is inscribed before me. . . .
>
> How can you say, "I haven't become defiled,
>   I haven't followed the Masters." (Jer 2:22-23; cf. Jer 13:27)

SHAMEFULNESS

Their behavior has thus been shameful, and it warranted a sense of shame like that of a man or woman who has been unfaithful in marriage. They have gone against the standards and values of their society and the standards and values approved by Yahweh.

First, as a matter of fact, their wrongdoing has been objectively shameful.

> The Shame has consumed
>   our ancestors' labor from our youth,
> Their flock and their cattle,
>   their sons and their daughters. (Jer 3:24)

"Shame" is *bosheth*. Now Saul had a son called Ishbosheth and a grandson called Mephibosheth, names that mean "man of shame" and "from the mouth of shame." It's hard to believe that they were their real names, and a plausible theory is that their real names were Eshbaal and Meribbaal. Maybe these names did not refer to Ba'al, the Master, but they sure look like it, and it seems that the names have been changed in the story to suggest how abhorrent such a name could seem. Sometimes a similar phenomenon appears in Jeremiah. He might have said "the Master" has consumed our ancestors' labor. Instead he says "the Shame" has done so (cf. Jer 11:13).

There's another, more subtle way in which Jeremiah can make the point. Another title for an alien god is "the king," *melek*, a title people could also properly apply to Yahweh. Applied to another god, then, it suggests something shameful. Jeremiah conveys the point simply by respelling the name. *Melek* becomes *molek*, replacing the word's proper vowels by the vowels of that word for shame. So Jeremiah can say, "They built up the shrines of the Master in the Ben-hinnom Ravine to make their sons and their daughters pass through the fire to the Shameful King" (Jer 32:35).

Therefore the Israelites are covered in shame—not just by a sense of shame but by an objective shamefulness. It happened when the Babylonians invaded Judah:

> We were shamed, because we heard reviling,
>> disgrace covered our faces.
> Because strangers came
>> into the sacred places in Yahweh's house. (Jer 51:51)

It has happened politically, and it will happen again politically, through their placing their trust in big powers rather than Yahweh.

> Through Egypt you'll be shamed again,
>> as you were shamed through Assyria.
> Through this you'll again come out
>> with your hands on your head. (Jer 2:36-37)

While shame is thus something objective, it is also, second, something subjective. The Israelites have recognized their shame, or they will come to do so.

> We must lie down in our shame,
>> our disgrace should cover us.
> Because we've done wrong to Yahweh our God,
>> we and our ancestors from our youth until this day.
> We haven't listened
>> to the voice of Yahweh our God. (Jer 3:25)

In the context of a drought, people look desperately for water and don't find any, and they are ashamed because they know the reason lies in their waywardness (Jer 14:3-4). The harvest fails, and the same response is appropriate (Jer 12:13).

Or, third, they are not ashamed when they should be.

> They've been shameful, because they've done something offensive;
>> they neither manifest any shame
>> nor do they know how to be disgraced. (Jer 6:15)

"You refused to be shamed" (Jer 3:3). In due course they will be.

MYSTERY AND STUPIDITY

In going after other deities and seeking support from people such as the Egyptians, Israel is strangely stupid as well as irresponsibly unfaithful. Jeremiah doesn't say that other gods don't exist or that Yahweh is the only supernatural being but rather that other supernatural beings have no power; they are useless (see "God in Christian Theology" in chap. 5 above), which makes Israel's attentiveness to them a mystery.

> They . . . were saying to a piece of wood, "You're our father,"
>   to some stone, "You gave me birth." . . .
>
> At the time when something bad happened to them
>   they'd say, "Arise, deliver us."
> But where are your gods
>   that you made for yourself?
> They should arise if they can deliver you,
>   at the time when something bad happens to you. (Jer 2:26-28)

Why Israel turned to the Master is a question the First Testament doesn't answer. One can make various guesses at answers. Perhaps worshiping the Master was more fun. Perhaps it was morally less demanding. The usual scholarly answer is that many Israelites had never turned to Yahweh in the first place. Jeremiah sees it simply as a mystery.

> The prophets prophesied by the Master,
>   and went after beings that couldn't prevail in anything. . . .
>
> Cross over to the shores of Kittim and see,
>   send off to Qedar and consider well,
>   see if something like this has happened.
> Has a nations changed its gods,
>   when those are not gods?
> But my people have changed my splendour
>   for what doesn't prevail in anything. . . .
>
> Two dire things my people have done:
>   me they have abandoned, the fountain of living water,
> To dig themselves cisterns, breakable cisterns,
>   ones that can't hold the water. (Jer 2:8-13)

The turning is a puzzle because on one hand Yahweh had proved himself as protector and provider, and on the other hand the Master couldn't deliver the goods. The Masters "couldn't prevail in anything" (Jer 2:8). Jeremiah can speak of the "Master" or the "Masters," perhaps because the one Master could have different names or identities as he appeared in different places, or perhaps because the plural expression serves as a term for deities in general.

Such alleged resources to which Israel turned were "empty," hollow, a mere breath (*hebel*). Nevertheless, people looked to them rather than to Yahweh as their resource. The empty nature of the gods means they are also the epitome of deception (Jer 3:23). Thus the prophets who prophesy through the Master (Jer 2:8) are prophesying by deception, and the priests follow them (Jer 5:31).

It just seems stupid. "My people are dense" (Jer 4:22). They have less sense than the birds in the heavens, they won't learn from the example of Ephraim, and they won't learn from what happened to Shiloh (Jer 3:6-10; 7:12-13; 8:7). They have eyes and ears but they don't use them (Jer 5:21).

SELF-INTEREST, GREED

While Yahweh's indictment chiefly concerns people's attitude to him, it also concerns people's attitude to one another, particularly the attitude and practice of people in positions of leadership. Such people fail to exercise authority in a truthful way, and their word cannot be trusted (Jer 5:1-3). The indictment can apply both to people in everyday positions of power such as the heads of households and to important people in the community (Jer 5:4-6) who "ought to know better," as we say. They have become rich and sleek, not through hard work or divine blessing but through duplicity. They've been like bird catchers setting traps for people (Jer 5:26-28). They ought to have been using their positions in the community to see that disputes were decided in a proper way. Maybe the head of a household has passed and someone else gets possession of his estate and displaces his family, or other needy people get into difficulty and lose their land. People with authority ought to be protecting the position of the fatherless and other needy people, but they aren't. Jeremiah can say of Jerusalem, "within it, all of it is fraud" (Jer 6:6).

Alongside the parable of the bird catcher, Jeremiah dreams up a caustic image for the fraudulence that powerful people practice on the fatherless and the needy. At Dan, in northern Israel, there bubbles up an astonishing flow of fresh cool water from Lebanon. It provides the Song of Songs with a picture of the beloved:

A garden spring,
> a well of living water,
> flowing from Lebanon. (Song 4:15)

A well that keeps water cool and refreshing on a hot day is a lovely picture. Jerusalem bubbles up too, but the water it is gushing is its dire behavior, its violence, and its destruction (Jer 6:6-7). In the Scriptures, there is improper violence and proper violence; Jeremiah's word (*hamas*) refers only to improper violence (it is not used of God's violence). It can denote violence in the sense of violation, but here it is accompanied by the word *destruction*. The city is full of destructive violence, of action that destroys people's lives, destroys the social and moral fabric of the city, and will soon destroy the city itself.

> From the smallest of them to the biggest of them,
>> everyone is grabbing what can be grabbed.
> And from prophet to priest,
>> everyone is practicing deception. (Jer 6:13)

They are greedy for loot and they are prepared to cheat and deprive other people of their rights so that they can fill their homes with good things. It applies to people of modest means and to people who have lots already—after all, you can never have enough, and you can never accept that some other people are better off than you. The same applies to prophets and priests, because ministers like nice homes too. So they are practicing deception—perhaps not least on themselves, certainly on one another, so that no one can trust anyone (Jer 9:3-9). If someone breaks into your house, you have an excuse for defending yourself and your family. They don't have that excuse.

> On your garments is found
>> the blood of the lives of needy people who are free of guilt
>> (you didn't find them breaking in). (Jer 2:34)

Leaders and Ministers

Whether or not the prophets and priests are involved in fraud, they are certainly involved in the deception that tells people things are going to be okay when they are not.

> From prophet to priest,
>> everyone is practicing deception.
> They have healed my people's shattering lightly,
>> saying "Things are perfectly well,"
>> when things are not well. (Jer 6:13-14).

Judah has had the experience of Pharaoh Neco killing Josiah and then deposing Jehoahaz and replacing him by Jehoiakim, but things are good now, the ministers say: they are "shalom shalom." Yahweh has taken his people through a rough patch, but he loves his people and will see that things are okay now. On the contrary, Jeremiah says, there is no shalom. Priests sometimes had the task of praying for people's healing and giving a judgment on whether healing was happening or whether there was risk of the sick or wounded person conveying defilement to other people; these priests are saying there is healing when there isn't. The prophets are giving people promises from God that he is not making. Deceiving people in this way constitutes the special offensiveness of leaders. The charge would be especially cutting for priests, who were supposed to make sure that nothing offensive compromised the sanctuary. The neglect of priests and prophets will mean that they as ministers have their special share in the shame that attaches to the entire community, and they will fall with them (Jer 6:15).

The ministers destine their people to horrific suffering because they don't acknowledge reality (Jer 14:18).

> The prophets prophesy falsely,
> > the priests rule on the basis of their own capacity,
> And my people like it so—
> > but what will you do at the end of it? (Jer 5:31)

Among the leaders were also the scribes, who might be the priests, though there were likely also non-priestly scribes.

> How can you say, "We are smart,
> > and Yahweh's instruction is with us"?
> Actually, there, it is for deception
> > that the scribes' pen of deception acts. (Jer 8:8)

We don't know which products of the scribes' pen Jeremiah refers to. It might be the writing down of priestly teaching and decisions, a process involved in the emergence of *the* Torah (Exodus to Deuteronomy), or the writing down of prophetic messages, as a scribe wrote down Jeremiah's messages. Either way, the reference to deception suggests that it was teaching or prophecy inspired by the Master rather than by Yahweh or produced in the name of a Yahweh who was so assimilated to the Master in the thinking of the priests or prophets that it was inspired by the Master even if the priests or prophets didn't realize it.

Teaching that has been put into writing, and recognized by Israel as having come from Yahweh, has the advantage of being fixed and unmalleable but also the disadvantage of being, well, fixed and unmalleable. It can't directly speak a word that relates to a new "now." It's one reason why prophets complement priests. The trouble is that prophets who claim to bring a message from Yahweh may be doing nothing of the sort; most of Jeremiah's references to prophets are to people whose word cannot be trusted.

The Septuagint translation and the Aramaic translation (the Targum) often translate the word for "prophets" by words meaning "false prophets," which they are, but Jeremiah simply calls them "prophets." They were not immediately distinguishable from the real thing; they did not go about wearing t-shirts that said "false prophet." Maybe they brought many messages that were true. But their key fault was to promise that Yahweh had good intentions for his people when he didn't. "I said, 'Oh! Lord Yahweh! There, the prophets are saying to them, "You won't see a sword, famine won't happen to you, because I shall give you true well-being in this place."' Yahweh said to me, 'It's falsehood that the prophets have prophesied in my name'" (Jer 14:13-14). The phrase "true well-being" puts together two key expressions; more literally, it denotes well-being characterized by truthfulness. "Well-being" is shalom (see "Well-Being" in chap. 6 above); the well-being the prophets are promising will be characterized by truthfulness or reliability (*'emet*). No, it won't, Yahweh says. They're making it up. It's wishful thinking. The fruit of their ministry will be that the people to whom they prophesy will come to a terrible end (Jer 14:16). So don't believe what your ministers say just because they are your leaders.

STUBBORNNESS

Jeremiah comments that an African can't change his skin color and a leopard can't change its spots (Jer 13:23). There is of course nothing wrong with being a black man or a spotted leopard, but you can't change it. Israel has taught itself so well to do wrong that it has lost the capacity to be different. To underscore the point, alongside the womanly image of Israel as an unfaithful wife, Jeremiah adds a male image. It's no good talking to them: their ear is foreskinned, they can't pay heed (Jer 6:10). It's a bizarre figure of speech, and a devastating one. A foreskin can get in the way of proper male functioning, and people similarly have something superfluous hanging over their ears that gets in the way of their hearing. So Jeremiah's speaking Yahweh's word to them is useless. It's not merely that they won't listen or won't take any notice. It's that they actively scorn and disparage it. Jeremiah keeps saying that disaster is coming, but they simply scorn his message. They are incapable of listening.

Elsewhere Jeremiah says that their mind—literally their heart—is foreskinned. As the ears stand for hearing, the heart stands for thinking, forming attitudes, and making decisions. Israel's attitude-forming and decision-making capacity is likewise inhibited by something hanging over their minds. Some other peoples around were circumcised as Israel was (Jer 9:25-26), and Israel could look askance at these other peoples who were foreskinned but only in a physical sense; they weren't circumcised in the way Israel was, with a circumcision that stood for Yahweh's pledge with them. Actually, Israel is no better than these other peoples—it is no more circumcised in mind than they are. To call Israel foreskinned (in hearing and mind) is in effect to say it doesn't belong to the people that Yahweh made his promises to. To put it another way,

> Judah's wrongdoing is written
>   with an iron pen,
> Engraved with a diamond point
>   on their mind's tablet. (Jer 17:1)

Jeremiah will later talk about Yahweh's expectations being written into people's minds (Jer 31:31-34), but at the moment their inclination to wrongdoing is engraved there, with a pen whose inscribing cannot be erased. Given that the mind is where attitudes are shaped and decisions made, its being engraved there has a decisive and irreversible effect on the shaping of behavior.

> The mind is more crooked than anything;
>   it's grave—who can know it?
> I am Yahweh, searching the mind,
>   testing the inner being,
> To give to an individual in accordance with his ways,
>   in accordance with the fruit proper to his practices. (Jer 17:9-10)

While the generalization is applicable to humanity as a whole, it is here a comment about Israel. The people engaged in defrauding the fatherless and needy can conceal their thinking from other human beings and they think they can conceal it from Yahweh. They are devious in a grave, grim, deep-seated way. But Yahweh has the capacity to look into the mind and inner being (literally, the heart and the kidneys) and thus to reward what he sees.

Jeremiah's initial indictment in Jeremiah 2–6 concludes with a summary in which Yahweh recapitulates the commission he gave Jeremiah in new words: Yahweh got him to examine Judah's paths (Jer 6:27). Really, Yahweh knew what he would find; the summary is designed for Judah to overhear. Yahweh also refers back to the charge he gave Jeremiah a little while previously

(Jer 5:1-6). Jeremiah's conclusions: they are "the most defiant of determined people, people who live as liars" (Jer 6:28). Yahweh has been engaged in smelting them, which works by adding lead to impure silver; the lead has the capacity to absorb the impurities from the silver. But the process hasn't worked. The impurity is still there in the silver, so it's no use.

> Reject silver, people would have called them,
> > because Yahweh has rejected them. (Jer 6:30)

The closing double use of the word *reject* constitutes a dreadful conclusion.

WRONGDOING IN CHRISTIAN THEOLOGY

There are several parallels between the way the New Testament speaks of wrongdoing and the way Jeremiah does. One is that it is a problem in the community as a whole. Like John the Baptizer, Jesus confronts the Jewish people of his day, though he takes a gentler stance to individuals. Paul likewise confronts congregations. A related comparison and contrast is that both see the entire world as characterized by wrongdoing and guilt and liable to have God take action against it, but Jeremiah thinks more in terms of nations, whereas Paul's "all have sinned" maybe thinks of people more individually. Another parallel is that Jesus, like Jeremiah, is especially aware of wrongdoing as characterizing the leadership of the people of God; it is a theme in Paul, though not quite as prominently.

A fourth parallel is more focused on big and occasional sins as opposed to smaller everyday sins—on the mortal more than the venial. In the church I attended as a teenager, we didn't confess our sins very often. I hadn't noticed or thought about the matter until a friend from another church came to worship with me and commented on it. Nowadays, as an Anglican, I say some version of the "general confession" twice a week from *The Book of Common Prayer*, along the following lines:

> Almighty and most merciful Father,
> we have erred and strayed from your ways like lost sheep.
> We have followed too much the devices and desires of our own hearts.
> We have offended against your holy laws.
> We have left undone those things that we ought to have done;
> and we have done those things that we ought not to have done;
> and there is no health in us.
> But you, O Lord, have mercy upon us sinners.

Spare those who confess their faults.
Restore those who are penitent,
according to your promises declared to mankind in Christ Jesus our Lord.
And grant, O most merciful Father, for his sake,
that we may hereafter live a godly, righteous and sober life,
to the glory of your holy name.

I don't think Jeremiah would have any problem with this prayer, but his stress on wrongdoing pushes us in a different direction. His emphasis is more like that of John the Baptizer. He presupposes that there are particular moments when the people of God have to face their wrongdoing in a serious fashion. Maybe he therefore would have no great problem with churches that don't routinely incorporate confession in their worship because they don't risk the trivializing of confession. But he would push us into facing the question of big sins in our relationship with God and with one another.

CHAPTER EIGHT

BEING A PROPHET

∴

PROPHECY IS AN IMPORTANT THEME IN JEREMIAH, more than in
any other prophetic scroll. One signal of its importance is the scroll's beginning with a detailed account of the period in which Jeremiah worked and
also with a vivid account of how Jeremiah came to be a prophet. These ac-
counts are not unique (one could compare them with Hosea and Ezekiel), but
they are unusual and significant, especially in light of the scroll's subsequent
focus on prophets and prophecy.

PARTY TO YAHWEH'S INTENTIONS

"Prophecy is difficult, especially with regard to the future," the proverb says.
As a prophet, Jeremiah operates with conviction on the basis of attending
meetings of Yahweh's cabinet, where he has voice but not vote. Yahweh's
cabinet is the meeting of Yahweh and his aides, the beings who act in the
world on Yahweh's behalf, who take part in the cabinet meeting on that basis.
It reflects the fact that Yahweh chooses not to do everything himself in the
world, like any not-too-self-centered leader, and not to decide everything
himself without consulting with his aides. They are the beings who can be
called gods with a lower-case *g*, supernatural entities who were created by
Yahweh as his envoys but who can also be thrown out and put to death by
Yahweh if they fail in their duties (see Ps 82). Some of them represent the
interests of different nations (who are then inclined to treat their god as if he

were God) in the cabinet discussions that make the decisions that they then are involved in implementing (see Dan 10). Being a prophet also means taking part in the cabinet meeting, both to speak on behalf of one's people (that's what intercession involves) and to learn of its decisions so as to pass them on (cf. also 1 Kings 22:19-23; Is 6; Amos 3:7-8). In spirit Jeremiah has taken part in those meetings and he therefore knows what he is talking about, but the other prophets haven't and don't.

> Because who has stood in Yahweh's council,
> and seen and listened to his word—
> who has heeded his word and listened? . . .
>
> I didn't send the prophets, but those people ran;
> I didn't speak to them, but those people prophesied.
> If they'd stood in my council,
> they'd have got my people to listen to my word.
> They'd have turned them back from their bad way,
> from the bad nature of their practices. (Jer 23:18, 21-22)

The problem with the other prophets in Jeremiah's day, who promised that things would go well with Judah and that Yahweh would look after his people, wasn't that they said things that were always wrong. The problem was that their day was a time when the cabinet had decided that things were to go badly. Prophets are people who recognize the time in which they live. They are able to do so if they recognize the truth about their people and because they take part in those meetings.

In Yahweh's commission, maybe the "this day" links with that necessity about being a prophet:

> See, I'm appointing you this day
> over the nations, over the kingdoms,
> To uproot and to pull down, to obliterate and to tear down,
> to build and to plant. (Jer 1:10)

One has some sympathy for Jeremiah in being overwhelmed by the idea of being "a prophet concerning the nations" (Jer 1:5). This feature in his vocation is not unparalleled in other prophets, but it applies to him in a special way because of the time in which he functions, the period of the transition from the Neo-Assyrian Empire to the Neo-Babylonian Empire, the time when the Babylonians will therefore be asserting themselves in countries like Judah, and the time when Yahweh will be losing patience with Judah as he lost patience with Ephraim.

Jeremiah will also function in time by having a message that concerns both uprooting and planting. It will be true for the nations in general, but his focus will be on Judah. One problem with being a prophet is that you have to say the opposite of what people believe. If people think things are fine, you have to say, "there's trouble on the way." If people think the situation is irreparable, you have to say, "be encouraged." For most of his ministry, Jeremiah will fulfill the first function. When the Jerusalem catastrophe is imminent and after it has happened, he will fulfill the second.

The chronological introduction to the scroll (Jer 1:1-3) also implies the need to recognize the time as it points to three chronological contexts for his ministry, which require three different messages. The time of Josiah is one where he can encourage the king in his reformation. The reign of Jehoiakim is one when he has to confront the king for going back on it. The arrival of Jerusalem's exile is the one when he can promise people that Yahweh will restore the city. Yahweh is consistent in his character and policies; the message doesn't change arbitrarily. But the dynamic of this arrangement shows that he needs to decide and say different things in different contexts. A prophet then needs to be someone who knows what God is saying now, which may be different from what he said yesterday or what he will say tomorrow. And people who read the prophets' words need to work with that dynamic.

The members of Yahweh's cabinet were not just participants in decision-making. They put the cabinet's decisions into effect. Prophets are also involved in this implementing. Yahweh bids Jeremiah to get hold of a pottery chalice and smash it, with a proclamation that Yahweh is going to smash people and city (Jer 19:1-15). While it provides a picture of what Yahweh intends to do, it also implements what Yahweh intends to do. A prophetic act functions a little like baptism, which both pictures death and resurrection or cleansing but is also God's means of bringing about death and resurrection or cleansing. Later, Yahweh gets Jeremiah to make yokes for Judah and its potential allies that match their submission to Babylon, and Jeremiah goes about wearing one for Judah (Jer 27:1–28:11). Hananiah breaks it, declaring that Yahweh is breaking the Babylonian yoke that Judah is wearing. Shalom prophets can also act out what they believe Yahweh is doing.

COMMISSIONED

To be in the cabinet meeting, you have to be summoned. Jeremiah relates how Yahweh's word came to him:

> Before I formed you in the womb I acknowledged you,
> > before you went out from the womb I made you sacred. (Jer 1:5)

It's common to speak of the vocation or call of a prophet, and there is one occasion when Jeremiah more or less uses this language: "your name was called out over me" (Jer 15:16). But the exception proves the rule. Calling one's name over something signifies ownership (Jer 7:10-11; 25:29). In Western thinking, discovering God's call implies discovering the vocation from God that matches who I am and that will enable me to find fulfillment as who I am while also serving God. Jeremiah's story gives no hint that he is finding fulfillment in that sense, and his account of his commission gives no hint of working in that framework. Maybe Yahweh's forming Jeremiah in the womb meant that he shaped Jeremiah to be the person who could fulfill the commission he had in mind, but Yahweh doesn't say so. He rather says that he "acknowledged" Jeremiah, an occasional First Testament expression for choosing someone for a special purpose. It applies to Yahweh's choice of Abraham and of Israel (Gen 18:19; Amos 3:2), which reflected not who they were but simply Yahweh's sovereignty. Thus in the parallelism of the wording, Yahweh can alternatively say that he made Jeremiah sacred. He claimed him as his own in the way he claims the Sabbath or the first of the harvest.

Maybe Jeremiah himself makes that Western assumption about vocation, that Yahweh chooses someone with the gifts that will match the vocation, in that he objects, "I don't know how to speak, because I'm a boy" (Jer 1:6). One need not assume he is still (say) a teenager; David calls his son Absalom a boy when he is old enough to have led a rebellion against his father, is trying to replace him as king, and has had sex with all his father's wives (2 Sam 18:5). But, anyway, Jeremiah has missed the point about the qualifications for being a prophet. Actually, there aren't any qualifications, at least in terms of eloquence. Yahweh provides the eloquence. "Yahweh put out his hand and touched my mouth, and Yahweh said to me: Here, I'm putting my words into your mouth" (Jer 1:9). In the ministry that follows, Jeremiah shows himself to be a poet and preacher of an eloquence that is exceeded by no other prophet and maybe equalled only by Hosea and Isaiah. It can hardly be that Yahweh simply put the words into his mouth because Yahweh did the same for other prophets who were less eloquent. So maybe Jeremiah didn't know himself and Yahweh did: he had the capacity to speak. But eloquence in itself doesn't mean you function satisfactorily as a prophet any more than lack of eloquence prevents it. Yahweh's response is therefore not, "Oh, you can do it." It's "the message comes from me, stupid" (cf. Jer 1:7-8).

Jeremiah needs to have both Yahweh's words and Yahweh's word. The word or message is the overall truth about Yahweh and his people, which Jeremiah understands but the other prophets don't.

> They're saying to people who disdain Yahweh's word,
>> "Things will go well for you."
> To everyone who's walking by the determination of his mind,
>> they've said, "Bad fortune won't come upon you." (Jer 23:17)

They don't recognize the basic truths about Yahweh and about ethics, and thus how the word or the message applies in a particular context. Jeremiah's membership of the cabinet means he knows the words or messages that need to be delivered to his people.

VULNERABLE BUT PROTECTED

If the vocation of a prophet is to say the opposite to what people think, a prophet is bound to be unpopular.

> You, you're to put your belt round your hips,
>> and get up and speak to them
>> anything that I myself order you.
> Don't shatter before them,
>> in case I shatter you before them.
> I—here I am, making you
>> into a fortified city today,
> Into an iron pillar
>> and copper walls against the entire country,
> For Judah's kings and its officers,
>> for its priests and the people of the country.
> They'll battle against you but they won't prevail over you,
>> because I'm with you (Yahweh's declaration) to rescue you. (Jer 1:17-19)

Jeremiah was a threat to priests who were giving people instructions that ignored the Torah, to experts who gave the king political advice based purely on political considerations, and to prophets who shared messages that came from their own imaginations. "Come on, we'll think up some intentions against Jeremiah," they therefore resolved, "because instruction won't perish from the priest, counsel from the smart person or word from the prophet. Come on, let's strike him down with the tongue, so we may not heed any of his words" (Jer 18:18).

How did the protection then work? In 609, at the beginning of Jehoiakim's reign, Jeremiah was in danger of being lynched. How did he escape? The story closes with the intriguing footnote, "the hand of Ahikam ben Shaphan was with Jeremiah so as not to give him into the people's hand to put him to death" (Jer 26:24). It looks as if Ahikam played a key role in the argument that the chapter records that led to Jeremiah's escape. The right person at the right time intervened on Jeremiah's behalf. The story makes no reference to Yahweh's involvement. On the other hand, the story of the 604 scroll also includes an intriguing side note: "The king ordered Jerahme'el the king's son, Seraiah ben Azri'el and Shelemiah ben Abde'el to get Baruch the secretary and Jeremiah the prophet, but Yahweh hid them" (Jer 36:26). How did Yahweh do it? It sounds as if there was something "miraculous" about their escape. But not surprisingly, Baruch was scared stiff, and Yahweh also promised him protection (Jer 45:1-5). He gave a similar promise to the African palace worker who rescued Jeremiah from likely death a few years later (Jer 38:1-13; 39:15-18). But it didn't work for everyone (see "Jeremiah 26–29 Begins: Think About the Reassuring Prophets" in chap. 4 above).

In a sequence of passages in Jeremiah 11–20, Jeremiah engages in exchanges with Yahweh about the cost of being a prophet. The traditional title for the passages is "confessions," but there is nothing confessional about them. They are more like protests. They arise from the reaction to Jeremiah's message from people in Judah, and not least in his hometown across the dividing line that marks Benjamin off from Judah (see "Jeremiah the Man" in chap. 1 above). Beyond the intervention of the right person at the right moment and the inexplicable quasi-miraculous escape, a key factor in Yahweh's protection is enabling Jeremiah to be aware of danger, such as the plots of people in Anathoth, whom Yahweh promises to sort out (Jer 11:18-23). "But why are you letting them behave like this?" Jeremiah responds (cf. Jer 12:1-4). "I'm not answering that question," Yahweh implicitly replies. "There's something else you need to think about. You think the pressure is bad. It's going to get worse. Get yourself mentally prepared" (cf. Jer 12:5-6).

Later, Jeremiah protests at Yahweh's having forced him into his ministry with the cost it brought to him, at the ridicule he had to endure for continually threatening people with a disaster that never came, at the impossibility of holding on to the threats instead of uttering them, and at the attacks he had to endure. But he closes his protest:

> Sing for Yahweh,
>> praise Yahweh.
> Because he's rescued the life of a needy person
>> from the hand of people who deal badly. (Jer 20:13)

Yes, he was vulnerable, but he was protected.

IDENTIFIED WITH YAHWEH

Jeremiah's commission is to deliver Yahweh's indictment of Judah and to give Judah notice that Yahweh intends to bring catastrophe on the people. He thus represents Yahweh. It is what makes his words like fire (Jer 5:14). But he didn't want to be the means of pouring out that fire.

> Yahweh's fury—I am full of it,
>> I am weary of holding it.

Okay, says Yahweh:

> Pour it on the baby in the street
>> and on the group of young people, altogether.
> Because man with woman, they are to be captured,
>> the old person with the one who is full of years.
> Their houses will pass to other people,
>> fields and wives, altogether.
> Because I will stretch out my hand
>> over the people who live in the country. (Jer 6:11-12)

If people want to attack Yahweh, they can do it by attacking Jeremiah. His question, "why does the way of the faithless succeed, why are all the people who break faith at ease?" (Jer 12:1), concerns not the general question of theodicy but why Yahweh does nothing about the waywardness of Judah and about their attacks on him.

> Oh, alas for me,
>> my mother, that you gave birth to me,
> An argumentative man and a disputatious man
>> for the entire country.
> Although I haven't lent and they haven't lent to me,
>> everyone slights me. (Jer 15:10)

He pays a price for his membership of the cabinet and his fulfilling his commission. Thus he begs,

> Grant me redress from my persecutors;
>> don't let me be taken, because of your long-temperedness.
> Acknowledge my bearing of reviling because of you;
>> your words presented themselves and I consumed them.
> Your word became joy to me,
>> the rejoicing of my mind.
> Because your name was called out over me,
>> Yahweh God of Armies.
> I haven't sat in the company of people having fun, and exulted;
>> because of your hand I've sat alone,
>> because you'd filled me with condemnation. (Jer 15:15-17)

Yahweh's response is typically tough.

> If you turn back, I'll let you come back;
>> you can stand before me. . . .
>
> Those people will turn back to you,
>> but you yourself won't turn back to them.
> To this people I shall make you
>> a copper wall, fortified;
> They'll battle against you
>> but not prevail over you.
> Because I shall be with you
>> to deliver you and to rescue you (Yahweh's declaration).
> I will rescue you from the hand of people who deal badly,
>> redeem you from the fist of the violent. (Jer 15:19-21)

A promise of that kind is significant, but it doesn't deal with the tension of his life. He has to keep delivering threats that he didn't make up and that Yahweh doesn't actually implement. When will Yahweh do as he says? (Jer 17:14-18).

IDENTIFIED WITH JUDAH

Yet Jeremiah will not be glad to see the people getting what they deserve. He will cry uncontrollably when they go off into exile (Jer 13:17). Indeed, he is already crying uncontrollably because he has seen the catastrophe in his imagination, seen the broken people, seen the corpses of people killed as the invading army approaches the city, and seen the famine-induced sickness in the city (Jer 14:17-18).

Because of my dear people's breaking I'm broken,
>   I mourn, devastation has taken strong hold of me.
Isn't there ointment in Gilead,
>   or is there no healer there?
Because why has my dear people's restoration
>   not developed?
If only my head were water,
>   my eye a fountain of tears.
I'd cry day and night
>   for those who are run through among my dear people. (Jer 8:21–9:1)

The last of the protests in the series of non-confessions proclaims:

Cursed be the day
>   on which I was born.
The day when my mother gave birth to me—
>   may it not be blessed. . . .

Why then did I go out from the womb
>   to see oppression and sorrow
>   and so my days might consume themselves in shame? (Jer 20:14, 18)

I take this protest as Jeremiah's climactic expression of identification with Judah, in which he declares the despair the city will be feeling once the catastrophe happens. If only they would think about it now.

We have noted that although Jeremiah doesn't have vote in the cabinet meetings, he does have voice. A prophet is an intercessor because he can plead on his people's behalf in these meetings. The reason why prayer matters is that it is the way one makes a contribution to cabinet discussions. If potential intercessors keep quiet, the cabinet will not decide to do what they might have asked. The reason why prayers sometimes get answered is that the cabinet sometimes agrees with them. The reason they don't get answered is that the cabinet sometimes has reasons for not agreeing with them. While Jeremiah doesn't see prayer as a battle (so prophets are not prayer warriors), he does suggest that prayer means taking part in an argument and in this sense "fighting" for the people one represents. If people like Hananiah are prophets and Yahweh's word is with them, "they should please intercede with Yahweh of Armies so that the rest of the things in Yahweh's house, in the house of the king of Judah, and in Jerusalem, don't come to Babylon" (Jer 27:18).

PRAYING AGAINST

Jeremiah has a number words for prayer, everyday words that then get applied to relationships with God. They suggest that prayer means:

- asking for grace, as Jeremiah once did of Zedekiah or people did of Jeremiah (Jer 37:20; 38:26; 42:2); asking for something that one does not deserve or has no right to (Jer 3:21; 31:9; 36:7; 42:9)
- intervening or interceding on behalf of someone else, like Jehoiakim's staff begging the king not to do something (Jer 36:25; see also Jer 7:16; 27:18)
- making a plea, as one does to a king as someone with the power to do as one asks, for oneself (Jer 29:12) or for other people (Jer 7:16; 11:14; 14:11; 29:7; 37:3; 42:2, 4, 20)
- seeking advice or some blessing for oneself (Jer 8:2; 10:21; 29:13; 37:7) or for someone else (Jer 21:2; 29:7; 30:14, 17; 38:4)

In his identification with Judah, Jeremiah prays,

> Pour your wrath on the nations that haven't acknowledged you,
>   on the kin-groups that haven't called out in your name.
> Because they've consumed Jacob,
>   consumed him and finished him off, and devastated his abode. (Jer 10:25)

This chilling prayer recalls the Psalms (e.g., Ps 137). It troubles people in the modern West, though Jeremiah is only asking Yahweh to do what he has said he intended to do (as is the case in Ps 137), and Jeremiah later conveys many declarations from Yahweh that imply a positive answer to this prayer (Jer 25:15-38; 46:1–51:64). In devastating Judah, a nation such as Babylon is implementing Yahweh's will. But Jeremiah takes into account that implementing Yahweh's will is not their aim. Their being the unintentional means of implementing Yahweh's will does not give them a free pass to set about furthering their imperial designs. They were devastating Judah because it suited them, not as an expression of their acknowledging Yahweh. And a little power like Judah is entitled to call on Yahweh to do something about it.

In a chilling protest on his own behalf, Jeremiah says:

> Is someone to make good with bad, for good?—
>   because they've dug a pit for me.
> Be mindful of how I stood before you
>   to speak good things concerning them,

to turn away your wrath from them.
Therefore give their children to famine,
    tip them out to the edges of the sword.
Their women should be bereaved of children and widowed,
    their men should be slain by death,
    their young men struck down by the sword in battle.
May an outcry make itself heard from their houses,
    when suddenly you bring a raiding gang on them.
Because they've dug a pit to capture me
    and laid snares for my feet.
Yahweh, you yourself know
    their entire counsel against me, for my death.
Don't expiate their waywardness,
    don't blot out their wrongdoing from before you.
They should become people caused to collapse before you;
    in the time of your anger, act against them. (Jer 18:20-23)

The Scriptures have no problem with this kind of prayer, which fits prayers in the New Testament (e.g., Rev 6:9-11), though again it troubles people in the modern West. It presupposes that there are no constraints on what you can say to God. There may be nothing else that children can do but cry out to their father, who is more powerful than they are; they are helpless. We might be glad that Jeremiah is praying rather than matching his attackers' assaults with assaults of his own.

PROPHETS IN CHRISTIAN THEOLOGY

In the New Testament, prophets appear in a series of ways:

- In the Gospels, the people who are explicitly called prophets are Anna (Lk 2:36-38), John the Baptizer (Mt 11:9), and Jesus (e.g., Lk 13:33).
- First Testament prophets such as Jeremiah help the Gospel writers understand Jesus (e.g., Mt 2:17) and ought to have helped people in Jesus' own time to do so (e.g., Lk 24:44).
- Acts also speaks of the activity of prophets in the churches (Acts 11:27; 13:1; 21:10), as does Paul (e.g., 1 Cor 14:29).

Jeremiah would hardly recognize what the New Testament does with his words, though he might recognize that the God who gave him his words could surely do what he liked with them in later contexts. Likewise, there seems no reason to think that Jeremiah would question the prophetic status of any of the people that the New Testament calls prophets, though many of them don't look very much like Jeremiah. But then within the First Testament, Gad or Haggai (among others) don't look much like Jeremiah either. A reading of the New Testament passages about prophets underscores how hard it is to say what a prophet is. And the way the ministry of prophets has continued recurrently in the church over the centuries has not reduced the difficulty of saying what a prophet is.

If one narrows the enquiry to asking what Jeremiah might imply regarding the questions to ask about prophets or purported prophets today, maybe some questions might be:

- do they say the opposite to what we think?
- does their message survive being measured by scriptural standards about behavior?
- do they hold together past, present, and future?
- do they get attacked by the people of God, and especially by its leaders?
- do they love the people of God?
- do they intercede?
- do they avoid making a profit out of being prophets?
- do they get martyred or miraculously rescued?
- is it hard to make sense of their message as a whole—does it seem inconsistent?
- do they combine threat and promise?
- does their message get rejected?
- do they persist, year in, year out?
- do they frighten us?
- are they independent of the structures (and payroll) of the people of God?
- are they offensive?
- do they speak poetically and act dramatically?

Jeremiah would invite a "yes" to these questions, though it would be unwise to take one or two of them out of the context of the whole.

CHAPTER NINE

THE FUTURE

"Days are coming," Yahweh says. It may be bad news (Jer 7:32; 9:25; 19:6; 48:12; 49:2; 51:47, 52) or good news (Jer 16:14; 23:5, 7; 30:3; 31:27, 31, 38; 33:14), and bad news for one may be good news for another. What you can be sure of is that the present and the past are not all there is. Yahweh is the God of the past and the God of the present but also the God of the future.

The Threat: Wrath, Redress, Devotion, Shame

At the climax of the first half of the Jeremiah scroll Yahweh gives Jeremiah a "chalice of wine (wrath)" to get Judah and other peoples to drink (Jer 25:15)—maybe it's spiked, or maybe it's just going to make them drunk. Either way, it will make them reel and flounder. The chalice stands for a sword that is to flail among the peoples. Initially Yahweh seems to imply that Nebuchadrezzar wields the sword, but in due course Babylon itself has to drink from the chalice. The sword assails "all earth's inhabitants" (Jer 25:29).

Yahweh does not say it is his sword, nor that the wrath is his, which opens up the possibility of seeing wrath as something objective and destructive, not necessarily an expression of someone's feelings. It points to something terrible happening that feels as if it must be an expression of someone's anger: the word suggests how it feels to a victim rather than a perpetrator. In this context, then, wrath needn't suggest that God feels angry; it denotes his doing the kind of thing that an angry person does. Something similar would apply to the idea of people "provoking" Yahweh (Jer 25:6-7). To provoke someone is to make them take action. Wrath and provocation needn't mean Yahweh *feels* wrathful.

But Yahweh does accumulate words for feelings such as *anger, fury,* and *great rage* (Jer 21:5). And backing away from that idea of God feeling anger is hard to fit with Jeremiah's other insights about God. God loves, gets angry, feels compassion, gets furious, grieves, gets enraged, and mourns. He has the same range of emotions as a human being, which is not surprising if we are made in God's image. If he had no feelings, would he be a living person? Jeremiah doesn't assume that there are good emotions (like compassion) and bad emotions (like anger). All emotions can be good or bad according to who the objects are and why. It's true of human beings, and it's true of God. The important thing to note is who God gets angry with, and what it results in.

Something similar applies to the idea of Yahweh taking redress (*neqamah*), which he may do on the basis of his people's unfaithfulness to him, their unfaithfulness to one another, or other peoples' wrongdoing (Jer 5:9, 29; 9:7-11; 50:15; 51:11). English translations use words such as taking vengeance, which gives the impression of overly irrational and vindictive action. Like wrath, redress is both rational and justified, and also strongly felt and fiery. Abandonment (e.g., Jer 9:2-3) carries the same two aspects. So perhaps does the tricky word for "devote" (*haram*). Devoting a piece of land or a donkey means giving it over to God, and you can't get it back. It becomes something given over to his service. But more often than not, devoting means killing. It mostly occurs as a metaphor for Israel's annihilation of foreign peoples in connection with entering into possession of Canaan. Jeremiah applies it to Babylon (Jer 50:21, 26; 51:3) but also to Judah, whom Yahweh means to devote and make "a devastation, something to whistle at, a complete waste permanently" (Jer 25:9). Making war on Jerusalem is thus a sacred task (Jer 6:4). "Devote" is usually a hyperbole; Israel didn't actually annihilate peoples. Yahweh doesn't annihilate Babylon or Judah. But inspiring Nebuchadrezzar to invade Judah did mean a lot of people lost their lives, and Yahweh recognizes that other peoples will be affected by the collateral damage.

Hyperbolically, this devastation will mean the collapse of creation (Jer 4:23-28). People need to use their imagination to have a sense of what it will be: it will resemble the agony of giving birth, the rape of a girl, the scattering of chaff, the exposure of an adulteress (Jer 13:21-27). Death will be climbing through people's windows (Jer 9:21). Shame, an objective reality even when not recognized (see "Shamefulness" in chap. 7 above), will become a visible one that people cannot evade. It will happen politically in connection with Judah's turning to Egypt (Jer 2:18-19, 36-37) and religiously in connection with Judah's turning away from "the fountain of living water" to empty alien deities (Jer 17:13). In a cutting turn of phrase, Yahweh makes a comparison between Moab's coming shame about their god Chemosh on whom they relied and Ephraim's shamed reliance on a god called Bet El (Jer 48:13).

CAN THE THREAT BE EVADED?

At his commission, Yahweh got Jeremiah to look at an almond tree, whose name happens also to mean "watcher," and declared,

> You've done good in looking,
> > because I'm watching, over my word, to put it into effect. (Jer 1:12)

The trouble is, this vision and conversation pairs with another, concerning a boiling pot facing from the north: "From the north bad things will open out on all the inhabitants of the country" (Jer 1:14).

"I shall make them a horror to all earth's kingdoms on account of Manasseh ben Hezekiah King of Judah, because of what he did in Jerusalem" (Jer 15:4). Are they paying the price for their parents' and grandparents' wrongdoing? In what sense is "this great bad fortune" coming "because your ancestors abandoned me"? But Yahweh goes on, "You've dealt badly more than your ancestors. There you are, following each of you the bad determination of his mind, so as not to listen to me" (Jer 16:10-12). Perhaps Yahweh would have pardoned the city if he had found one truthful person there, but he couldn't (Jer 5:1).

If you were feeling bold and cynical, like some Judahites Jeremiah mentions, you might tell yourself that Yahweh is all talk and no action. But you might be wiser to ask what action you need to take. The key verb in this connection is "turn." Turning means (for instance) acknowledging Yahweh truly; removing abominations; exercising faithful authority; circumcising your thinking; washing your mind; fulfilling the Ten Commandments; relying on Yahweh rather than other human or supernatural resources (e.g., Jer 3:1–4:17; 7:5-7; 17:5-8). Perhaps then people's prayer for grace will fall before Yahweh and he will pardon their waywardness (Jer 36:2-3, 7).

Yahweh does urge Judah to turn back to him, as if it can then avert calamity (see "Jeremiah 18–20 Begins: Think About God's Sovereignty" in chap. 3 above), while also speaking as if set on bringing catastrophe to Judah. Might the exhortation belong to one stage in Jeremiah's ministry and the declaration to another stage when turning is no longer possible? While the account of Jeremiah's commission already speaks of that pot boiling over from the north, as if it is inevitable, twenty years later in the reign of Jehoiakim no disaster has happened. Yahweh is again threatening it but still hoping that Judah might turn back (Jer 26:3; 36:3, 7). He continues issuing threats for nearly another two decades before actually having Jerusalem devastated.

After the 597 exile, Jeremiah likens the Jerusalem community to a basket of bad figs, and the people taken off to Babylon in 597 to good figs (Jer 24:1-10). He doesn't say that the Babylon community *are* good figs, as if to imply that the faithful people had been taken into exile and the unfaithful were the ones left behind. To judge from everything else that he says, there was nothing to choose between different people, families, and groups in Judah; he is especially rude about King Jehoiachin who was taken off with other leading figures in 597. His point rather is that good figs have a future, while bad figs don't. Whereas the Jerusalem community would indeed be tempted to think that the people taken off to Babylon are people Yahweh thereby designated as especially deserving exile and having no future, Yahweh's point is that the Jerusalem community needs to see itself as having no future (if the Babylon community should be subsequently inclined to use this message to support a claim to be the people with the future over against the people left in Judah, they have missed Yahweh's point). The implication is not despair. In about the same context, Jeremiah challenges Zedekiah: "Bring your necks to the king of Babylon's yoke, serve him and his people, and live" (Jer 27:12). More or less halfway through Zedekiah's reign and halfway between the 597 exile and the 587 exile, Jeremiah again issues the same exhortation (Jer 28:1-14). Only in the context of the final siege does Jeremiah speak as if the city's fall is inevitable (Jer 34:1-7). Yahweh's face is now definitively set against the city and the challenge is for individuals to take action if they don't want to be swallowed up by the event. Abandoning the city and surrendering to Nebuchadrezzar is "the way of life" as opposed "the way of death" (Jer 21:8).

WILL THE DEVASTATION BE CONSTRAINED?

If there is no turning, Yahweh can speak as if he intends simply to destroy Judah; nothing will remain. The northern forces will attack Judah like people harvesting grapes, which is a devastating experience for the grapes, but the Torah's rules require harvesters not to be too thorough but to leave something behind for needy people. One could say that Israel has already been well and truly "harvested": only little Judah is left as the remainder of what the nation once was. But,

> Like a vine they are to glean and glean
> > the remainder of Israel.
> "Put your hand again
> > like a grape-picker over the branches." (Jer 6:9)

The traditional translation of the word for "remainder" (*she'erit*) is "remnant"; eventually it becomes a significant theological term. Here it just means the grapes that were left after the first brisk harvesting that might have been left for needy people. It won't happen. The vine is to be left totally bare. There will be no remnant.

Yet Jeremiah has already said things that clash with that idea: "The entire country will become desolation (but I won't make an end)" (Jer 4:27; cf. Jer 5:18). He has even used the vine image in this connection:

> Go up among its vine-rows and destroy them,
> > but don't make an end.
> Remove its branches,
> > because those people don't belong to Yahweh. (Jer 5:10)

Did Yahweh intend total destruction and then have a change of mind? Would the order of the chapters rather imply that he intended incomplete destruction, then changed his mind in favor of total destruction, then changed his mind again and didn't do it? Has he simply not made up his mind yet? Or does he think one thing on Sunday, Tuesday, and Thursday and another on Monday, Wednesday, and Friday (we know that Saturday is his day off)? That would be logical, because there are considerations that point in both directions.

In between some of the qualified threats, Jeremiah has already observed to Yahweh, "you finished them off" (Jer 5:3), though he goes on, "but they refused to accept discipline," which indicates that they still existed and that Jeremiah was being hyperbolic. If he told Judah that the destruction would not be total, would he be compromising his threat's effectiveness? Was the threat of total destruction always hyperbolic? Total devastation would be appropriate and necessary given the total depravity Jeremiah portrays (though sometimes it is hyperbolic, as in the case of Baruch and the people who appear in Jer 26:16-24, because there are exceptions to his rule). "I shall not pity and I shall not spare and I shall not have compassion so that I don't devastate them"

(Jer 13:14). "I have gathered up my well-being from this people (Yahweh's declaration), my commitment and compassion" (Jer 16:5).

But total devastation would also be impossible given Yahweh's unconditioned commitment to Israel (cf. Paul's argument in Romans 9–11). Only if the movements of sun, moon, stars, and tides cease, "Israel's offspring may also cease from being a nation for all time," and only if human beings may get the measure of the heavens and the earth's foundations "I may reject the entire offspring of Israel for what they've done" (Jer 31:36-37).

> I am with you (Yahweh's declaration) to deliver you,
>> because I shall make an end among all the nations
>> where I've scattered you,
> Yet of you I won't make an end,
>> though I discipline you in exercising authority
>> and don't treat you as free of guilt. (Jer 30:11)

The formulation is subtle: "an end among all the nations" but "of you I won't make an end."

It seems that Yahweh has boxed himself into a corner. Did some of Jeremiah's curators write the bits about complete devastation and different ones write the bits about partial devastation? That theory doesn't help because the scroll still embraces both, and both have good theological and ethical rationales. Rather, Yahweh is boxed into a corner by two truths that stand in tension with each other. Both have to be respected.

WILL THE TIME OF DEVASTATION BE CONSTRAINED?

Judah asks, rhetorically,

> Does he hold on to things permanently
>> or keep watch for all time? (Jer 3:5)

Yahweh can suggest the answer "yes":

> I shall make you serve your enemies
>> in a country that you haven't known.
> Because you've lit a fire in my anger
>> that will burn permanently. (Jer 17:4; cf. Jer 18:15-16)

On the other hand, he can offer the assurance to people who will "come back" that "I shall not make my face fall against you, because I am committed

(Yahweh's declaration), I don't hold on to things permanently" (Jer 3:12). After all, "with permanent love I loved you" (Jer 31:3).

To make the tension between the two truths more complicated, if they turn their backs on their waywardness, "I'll let you dwell in this place, in the country that I gave to your ancestors from of old, permanently" (Jer 7:7). Excuse me, if he gave it permanently, how can he now say "if" in that way? Again, it will be if they turn their backs on their waywardness that "there will come through this city's gateways kings and officials sitting on David's throne, riding on chariots and horses, they and their officials, Judah's people and Jerusalem's inhabitants. This city will stay permanently" (Jer 17:25). But didn't he make a permanent promise to David? Again, "I shall *devote* them and make them a devastation, something to whistle at, a complete waste permanently. . . . But when seventy years are fulfilled, I shall attend to the king of Babylon and to that nation (Yahweh's declaration) for their waywardness, to the country of the Chaldeans, and make it a desolation permanently" (Jer 25:9, 12).

If people turn, then Yahweh can pardon and devastation can be averted (Jer 36:3). If there is no turning and devastation happens, there can then be compassion and pardon (Jer 30:18; 31:34; 33:8). When the people of God are avoiding the unpleasant facts, they need to be faced with them. But there comes a time when shalom is God's message. "Days are coming (Yahweh's declaration) when I shall restore the fortunes of my people Israel and Judah," (Jer 30:3; see "Jeremiah 30–33 Begins: Think About Restoration and Returning" in chap. 4 above). "Days are coming (Yahweh's declaration) when I shall sow Israel's house and Judah's household with human seed and animal seed. As I was watchful over them to uproot, to demolish, to tear down, to obliterate, and to deal badly, so I'll be watchful over them to build and to plant" (Jer 31:27-28). Yes, "his commitment lasts permanently" (Jer 33:11). "Yahweh has said this (Yahweh is going to do it, he's going to form it, he is going to make sure of it—Yahweh is his name): 'Call to me and I shall answer, and tell you great things, secret things that you haven't acknowledged'" (Jer 33:2-3).

To the 597 exiles, therefore, he says:

> At the bidding of the fulfillment for Babylon of seventy years I shall attend to you, and act for you on my word about good things, bringing you back to this place. Because I myself acknowledge the intentions that I'm formulating for you (Yahweh's declaration), intentions for your well-being and not for bad things, to give you a future, a hope. You will call me and come and plead with me and I shall listen to you. You will seek me and find me if you inquire of me with your

entire mind, and I'll be able to be found by you (Yahweh's declaration). I shall restore your fortunes, collect you from all the nations and from all the places where I've driven you (Yahweh's declaration) and bring you back to the place from where I've exiled you. (Jer 29:10-14)

THE RESTORATION AND THE PLEDGE

Therefore, Jeremiah 30–33 promises, the future of the people of God will be

- genuine in their relationship with God
- reunited in its relationship with God: the people who turned away will turn back
- a people for Yahweh, as he will be God for them
- numerous, a great congregation
- communal in its relationship with God, embracing both Judah and Ephraim, "all Israel's clans," young and old together
- national and freed from the sovereignty of other overlords but accepting dependence on Yahweh
- governed by its own rulers
- geographically located, in Canaan
- gathered back as the flock that was scattered
- collected from the farthest reaches of the earth, blind and lame, pregnant and in labor
- provisioned on the journey
- urban, the city of Jerusalem being rebuilt as a place where there are homes for people and as a place from which proper authority can be exercised and the powerless protected
- agrarian and pastoral, rejoicing over grain, new wine, fresh oil, new born of flock and cattle
- honored rather than shamed
- healed of its wounds
- worshipful, joyful, celebratory, reveling, dancing, and never sorrowing again
- purified from waywardness and pardoned for rebellion
- tractable, with Yahweh's expectations written into his people's minds, a single mind and a single way, living in awe of Yahweh

- realistic: not sinless, but with the problems in the relationship resolved in the present
- secure and confident, calm, and at peace
- living by Yahweh's pledge that he will not turn back from them, and with his delight in them
- no longer turning away from him

They will no longer say, "The parents ate sour grapes but the children's teeth feel rough." Rather, each person will die for his waywardness. Everyone who eats sours grapes, his teeth will feel rough.

"There, days are coming (Yahweh's declaration) when I will solemnize with Israel's household and with Judah's household a new pledge, not like the pledge that I solemnized with your ancestors on the day I took strong hold of them by the hand to get them out of the country of Egypt, my pledge which they contravened, though I was master over them (Yahweh's declaration). Because this is the pledge that I shall solemnize with Israel's household after those days (Yahweh's declaration). I'm putting my instruction inside them and I shall write it on their mind; and I'll be God for them and they'll be a people for me. They will no longer teach each person his neighbor and each his brother, saying 'Acknowledge Yahweh,' because all of them will acknowledge me from the least of them to the biggest of them (Yahweh's declaration), because I shall pardon their waywardness, and their wrongdoing I shall not keep in mind anymore." (Jer 31:29-34)

DAVID AND LEVI

David and Levi need to feature in Yahweh's promises for the future. There is a practical reason—that Israel needs leaders in national life, community life, political life, and worship life. The other reason is that Yahweh made commitments to these lines of national leaders and worship leaders.

"Hey, shepherds who led astray and scattered my flock (Yahweh's declaration)." Therefore Yahweh, Israel's God, has said this about the shepherds who shepherd my people: "You—you've let my flock scatter. You've driven them away and not attended to them. Here am I; I'm going to attend to you, to the bad nature of your practices (Yahweh's declaration). And I myself will draw together the remainder of my flock from all the countries where I've driven them. I'll take them back to their abode, and they'll be fruitful and become many. I'll set up shepherds over them and they'll shepherd them, and they won't be afraid any more or shatter or be missing." (Jer 23:1-4)

God made magnificent promises to David, about him and his sons ruling in Jerusalem for all time (2 Samuel 7). Another tension emerges, and another dilemma. The promises put Yahweh in a tricky position when the Davidic king doesn't exercise authority faithfully. Does he stay faithful to his promises and turn a blind eye? Or does he prioritize the importance of the faithful exercise of authority and let David's household fall? Yahweh finds a way through the dilemma by abandoning David's household in the short term but making a commitment to it for the long term. He lets Jehoiachin and then Zedekiah be deposed and taken into exile but confirms the long-term commitment in a promise that follows the critique of these kings (see "Jeremiah 21–25 Begins: Think About Government" in chap. 3 above).

> I shall set up for David a faithful branch. He will reign as king and show insight and exercise authority and faithfulness in the country. In his days Judah will find deliverance and Israel will dwell with confidence. This is the name by which he'll be called: "Yahweh Is Our Faithfulness." Therefore, here, days are coming (Yahweh's declaration) when they will no longer say "As Yahweh lives, who got the Israelites up from the country of Egypt." Rather, "As Yahweh lives, who got up and brought the offspring of Israel's household from the northern country" and from all the countries where I will have driven them. And they will live on their land. (Jer 23:5-8)

The usual image for David's line is a household, but here the promise begins from the picture of David's line as a tree. The tree is being felled, so there will be no Davidic king. Outside our apartment, there are two giant old trees that were savagely cut back last year. We could not imagine them growing again, and we have been astounded at the new growth that we have seen. Yahweh can make a branch grow even from a tree that has been felled. This "branch" will be a king who lives up to the job description. It will bring the blessing for the people that good leadership is supposed to bring. Jeremiah closes the promise in marvelously sardonic fashion. The name of this king will be "Yahweh is our faithfulness," *Yahweh Zidkenu.* Now Zedekiah's own name means "Yahweh is my faithfulness." If only it had been true. This new king will live up to the name. When the First Testament gives someone a name in this way, it need not mean it is the name that people use in everyday life. Matthew 1:23 quotes Isaiah 7:14 including the words, "they shall name him Emmanuel," whereas we already know that he is to be called Jesus, but this other "name" indicates something of his significance. So it is with some First Testament names, especially ones that are more like phrases or sentences. This coming of this new king will be an expression of the fact that "Yahweh is our faithfulness."

There was a divine commitment to Levi too and a need of people to lead in worship. Alongside the renewed promise to David, then:

> From the priests, the Levites, there will not be cut off someone before me offering up the whole offering and burning the grain offering and performing the sacrifice, for all time. . . .
>
> If you people can contravene my pledge about the day and my pledge about the night so that there's no day and night at their time, also my pledge with David my servant may be contravened so that there's no son for him reigning on his throne, and with the Levites, the priests, ministering to me. As the heavens' army cannot be counted and the sea's sand cannot be measured, so I shall multiply the offspring of David my servant and the Levites who minister to me. (Jer 33:18-22)

LIVING IN BETWEEN

The temple was rebuilt after the exile, and for six centuries Levites functioned there in fulfillment of Yahweh's promise; we have noted the significance of Zechariah (Lk 1) as an embodiment of it. But soon after his day, Jerusalem was destroyed again, and no Levites have made offerings since then. The Davidic promise saw thinner fulfillment. There has been no Davidic king since Jehoiachin and Zedekiah. God has continued to occupy a middle ground between acting as he said to David and abandoning his promise. Jehoiachin's grandson Zerubbabel ruled in Judah, though as administrator or governor (*pehah*), not as king (Hag 1–2). In the second century BC, Judah had kings, but they were not descendants of David. Jesus was David's descendant, but he did not reign as king in the straightforward sense and he was not in a position to exercise authority with faithfulness, though Jesus as a metaphorical king was a better fulfillment than any literal king could have been. But the implementing of faithful authority remains a commitment that we have to pray to God to bring about in the world. Jesus could not be a fulfillment of the promise to Levi because he belonged to the wrong clan, though he did facilitate the worship and service of the people of God in a way that fulfilled Levi's vocation. As a result of his death and resurrection, Paul can realistically urge a Jewish and Gentile body in Rome to offer themselves as a living sacrifice to God in an act of religious service (*latreia*) that involves mind as well as body (it is *logikos*).

"Occupying middle ground" is then the wrong image. Doing better than one promised is more than fulfillment, not a failure of fulfillment.

There is a link between these considerations and the final chapter of the Jeremiah scroll. Jeremiah 52 talks about ends and beginnings and about living in between. Jeremiah 39 has already told the story of the fall of Jerusalem that Jeremiah 52 retells, but each telling fulfills a function in its context in the scroll, and there are differences in the retold version. It omits the transition into the creating of a possible continuing community (which turns out to be abortive) and adds some surprisingly small figures for the number of people Nebuchadrezzar forced into migration. It then closes with a note from 562, a quarter-century later, about the release of the former king Jehoiachin from house arrest and his being given a position of honor in the Babylonian court. This close to the scroll's narrative gives it a hopeful ending without changing the devastating nature of the story that relates the fulfillment of Jeremiah's nightmares about the city's fall. Thus the story told for the benefit of people living in the mid-sixth century conveys the mixed message that matches their situation. They live with the aftermath of a terrible sequence of events, but they live with evidence that Jeremiah was right (he is presumably dead by now): Yahweh is not finished with them. Another quarter-century later, Cyrus the Persian will conquer Babylon and encourage the Judahites there to go home and rebuild the temple, and provide more spectacular evidence that Jeremiah was right and that Yahweh is not finished with them:

> In the first year of Cyrus King of Persia, fulfilling Yahweh's word from the mouth of Jeremiah, Yahweh stirred the spirit of Cyrus King of Persia, and he made an announcement pass through his entire kingdom, and also in writing: Cyrus King of Persia has said this:
>
> > Yahweh the God of the heavens has given me all the kingdoms of the earth, and he himself has appointed me to build him a house in Jerusalem, which is in Judah. Whoever among you from all his people: may his God be with him, and may he go up to Jerusalem which is in Judah and build the house of Yahweh the God of Israel. (Ezra 1:1-3)

The prayer in Daniel 9 will take up Jeremiah's seventy years prophecy in another context and wonder about the same tension between prophecy and fulfillment and living now. The people of God continually live between God's promises (and threats) and their final fulfillment, accepting and trusting that moments that can be seen as interim fulfillments encourage and warn them to live in light of eventual final fulfillment.

THE FUTURE IN CHRISTIAN THEOLOGY

Christian theology has often seen prophecy such as Jeremiah as foretelling—it reveals God's intentions that he fulfilled in Jesus. The death of the Bethlehem babies reminds Matthew of Jeremiah's words about Rachel crying (Mt 2:17), while the New Testament makes substantial appeal to Jeremiah in seeing Jesus as implementing the promise of a new pledge or covenant (Heb 8–10).

I imagine that Jeremiah would have no problem with the New Testament using his words to help it understand Jesus but that he might make two further comments. One is that he would like us not to lose the significance of the words Yahweh gave him for his people in his own day. When the Jewish people or the church are in exile, Rachel weeps over them and God listens to her crying and responds. When Jeremiah passed on the promise of a new pledge, it not only anticipated something God would do for people in six centuries time but spoke to people in the sixth century about something God would do for them. And he fulfilled his pledge to them in renewing his covenantal relationship and inscribing his expectations into his people's thinking, so that after the exile they lived by the Decalogue's commands about serving only Yahweh, abjuring images, revering his name, and keeping the Sabbath, as they had not before. Conversely, Hebrews speaks hyperbolically about the effect of Jesus' death and resurrection. It is not obvious that people who believe in Jesus live out the promise of the new covenant any more than Jews who do not trust in Jesus, as if God's expectations of us are inscribed into our minds and lives and we don't need to teach or encourage each other to know or acknowledge God. It's still the case that we live "in between." We have more evidence that Jeremiah spoke truly than people had in 604 or 587 or 562 or 539, but we still live in between the confirmation of God's promises in Jesus and their final fulfillment.

Jeremiah might also draw our attention to the small number of his words that the New Testament quotes as fulfilled in Jesus. It doesn't even quote Jeremiah 23:5-8. But even if it had done so, the thinness of its references indicates that the Jeremiah scroll contains little by way of messianic prophecy. For Jeremiah as for other prophets, foretelling the Messiah is not a prominent concern. Conversely, again, Jeremiah might be concerned about streams of Christian theology and spirituality that downplay the wrath of God. While it is an important theme in Jeremiah, Romans and Revelation have more references per page, and there are a number of ways of misunderstanding it. But the New Testament works with the same awareness that there is something objective and impersonal about it, and something subjective and personal. It is almost as if they had read Jeremiah.

The consideration about messianic prophecy leads into a reflection on the alternative inclination of Christian theology to see prophecy such as Jeremiah as forthtelling more than foretelling—it tells forth God's expectations of his people and of the world. Again, I imagine Jeremiah would have no problem with this insight, but he might make two further comments. No, he was not telling people about things to happen in hundreds of years' time, as if God revealed in 2000 things to happen in 2500 (he could do so, but it would be odd). He did tell people about things that would happen in their lifetime or their children's or grandchildren's lifetime ("seventy years"). He didn't just tell people what they should do. He told them what God was going to do, for ill and for good. The other comment would be that the focus of his forthtelling was people's attitude and life in relation to God, in the trust expressed (or not expressed) in their worship and their politics, more than their commitment to social justice. Jeremiah knows that Yahweh is the real God and that he is involved in his people's lives, and he urges his people to live their lives on that basis.

FURTHER READING

My commentary:
Goldingay, John. *Jeremiah*. NICOT. Grand Rapids, MI: Eerdmans, 2021.

Some other commentaries that are not too technical that I have found illuminating:

Brueggemann, Walter. *A Commentary on Jeremiah: Exile and Homecoming*. Grand Rapids, MI: Eerdmans, 1998.

Calvin, John. *Commentary on Jeremiah and Lamentations*. Reprint. Carlisle, PA: Banner of Truth, 1989.

Fretheim, Terence. *Jeremiah*. Smith and Helwys Bible Commentary. Macon, GA: Smith and Helwys, 2002.

Jerome. *Commentary on Jeremiah*. Ancient Christian Texts. Translated by Michael Graves. Edited by Christopher A. Hall. Downers Grove, IL: IVP Academic, 2011.

Miller, Patrick. "Jeremiah." *The New Interpreter's Bible* 6:553-926. Nashville: Abingdon, 2001.

Stulman, Louis. *Jeremiah*. Abingdon Old Testament Commentaries. Nashville: Abingdon, 2005.

Tyler, Jeffrey J., ed. *Jeremiah, Lamentations*. Reformation Commentary on Scripture. Downers Grove, IL: IVP Academic, 2018.

Wright, Christopher. *The Message of Jeremiah*. Bible Speaks Today. Downers Grove, IL: IVP Academic, 2014.

SUBJECT INDEX

SCRIPTURE INDEX

Finding the Textbook You Need

The IVP Academic Textbook Selector
is an online tool for instantly finding the IVP books
suitable for over 250 courses across 24 disciplines.

_____

ivpacademic.com

_____